KU-194-419

GATEWAY GUIDE TO

SPAIN

A LITTLE ABOUT THE COUNTRY · HISTORY

ART AND ARCHITECTURE

NATIONAL FESTIVALS AND RECREATIONS

THE LANGUAGE · SOME USEFUL SPANISH WORDS

PREPARING FOR THE TRIP · HOW TO GET TO SPAIN

WHAT IS THE FARE? · TRAVELLING IN SPAIN

STAYING THE NIGHT · WHAT TO EAT

MADRID · BARCELONA · TOLEDO

18 TOURS THROUGH SPAIN

METHUEN & CO LTD
36 ESSEX STREET : STRAND : LONDON WC2

GATEWAY GUIDE TO SPAIN

Illustrated by Ib Withen

CONTENTS

IN THE SAME SERIES

Austria; Belgium and Luxembourg; England; France; Germany
Holland; Italy; Switzerland; Paris; Rome; Costa Brava;
Majorca and Ibiza

CATALOGUE NO. 2/5772/29

First published in Denmark by POLITIKENS FORLAG

First published in English 1958

Reprinted with corrections and brought up to Date 1962

Copyright in all countries signatory to the Berne Convention

English Translation © *1958 by Methuen & Co. Ltd*

PRINTED IN GREAT BRITAIN BY
BUTLER AND TANNER LTD, FROME AND LONDON

An everyday scene in one of Spain's lovely old towns, Toledo: the strongly fortified St Martin's Bridge, which spans the River Tagus

AREA AND POPULATION

The land beyond the *Pyrenees*, the *Iberian peninsula*, measures 225,200 sq. miles. Of this the area of *Spain* is 190,700 sq. miles, while that of *Portugal* is 34,500 sq. miles, and the *Balearic Islands* consist of 1935 sq. miles. The population of mainland Spain is about 30,245,000 making an average density of 154 per sq. mile, whereas Portugal with its small population of about 8,700,000 has nearly twice the average density, 251 per sq. mile, and the Balearic Islands have a density of 234 per sq. mile with their population of about 448,000.

LANDSCAPE

The Pyrenees form the Franco-Spanish frontier; and the rest of the landscape is one of mountains and plateaux. The Pyrenees continue westwards as the *Cantabrian Mountains*: these completely cover *Asturias* and *Galicia* and together with the *Sierra de Gata*, the *Sierra de Gredos*, the *Sierra de Guadar-*

rama, and the *Iberian Border Mountains* enclose *Old Castile*. La Mancha, the plateau south of *Madrid*, is also framed by mountains: the *Sierra Guadarrama*, the *Toledo mountains*, the *Sierra Morena* and the *Sierra Grillemona*. Further south, on the coast, is the beautiful range of the *Sierra Nevada*, with the highest mountain of the Iberian peninsula, the *Pico de Mulhacen* (11,420 ft.).

RIVERS

The five largest rivers in Spain are: the *Ebro*, which rises in the Cantabrian mountains and flows into the Mediterranean between Barcelona and Valencia; the *Duero*, rising in the Iberian Border Mountains, flows through old Castile and Portugal (where it becomes the *Douro*) into the Atlantic near Oporto; the *Tajo* or *Tagus* comes from the Sierra de Cuenca, passes Toledo and flows into the Atlantic at Lisbon; the *Guadiana* also rises in the Cuenca mountains, flows right across the plateau of La Mancha and

Mountains and rivers in Spain

INDUSTRY AND AGRICULTURE

Spain is first and foremost an agricultural land, but the methods of farming are predominantly old-fashioned; progress has been slight until more recent years. A good 15% of the land is barren and much of it which is fertile either lies fallow or is used as pasture. Irrigation is a great problem in many places. Wheat, rye, oats, barley, onions, rice, potatoes and cotton are grown, also vines, olives, almonds, lemons, oranges and a few crops of lesser importance, such as figs, dates, flax, cork, carrots and sugar-beet. Live-stock farming is of little importance, except for some sheep-breeding and the raising of bulls for the national spectacle—bull-fighting. There was little forestry until recently, but this has made great strides since 1950. The cork-oak is important and grows wild in the *Estremadura*, being heavily cultivated in the province of Gerona for both national requirements and export.

Spanish soil is rich in minerals; coal, iron, zinc and copper are the most important.

Industry is expanding here as in other lands. Textiles, leather goods, tinned fish, fruit and foodstuffs are the main products.

THE CONSTITUTION

General Franco leads the country as Head of the State, Commander-in-Chief of the Army, and leader of the Falange—the country's only political party. Since 1942 the 'Cortes' has functioned once more as the law-giving assembly.

Franco, according to his own declaration in 1947, considers himself to be the head of state or Regent for a monarchy, and after his death a regency-council will appoint his successor, if he has not already done so, possibly a member of the Spanish royal family.

continues through the Estremaduras highland until, with a sharp swerve to the south on the Portuguese frontier, it flows into the Atlantic in the Gulf of Cadiz. The largest river is the *Guadalquivir*. Its source is in the Sierra de Segura, and it drains Andalusia, flowing past Cordoba and Seville, before joining the sea near Cadiz.

CLIMATE

As Spain is a large country, the climate varies greatly in different parts. An imaginary line from *Lisbon* through *Madrid* and *Zaragoza* to *Barcelona* roughly divides the peninsula into the northern temperate and the southern sub-tropical zones. South of this line day frost is practically unknown and the summers are extremely hot and dry. Some average temperatures:

Place	January	July
Barcelona	44°	73°
Bilbao	47°	69°
Madrid	40°	76°
Seville	58°	85°

The Atlantic coastal region has a marked coastal climate: comparatively cool in summer and mild in winter. It has plentiful rain, especially in winter. On the Mediterranean coast the climate is more or less the same as that of the French Riviera: warm all the year with very slight rainfall. In Central Spain temperatures can rise to over 100° in summer.

HISTORY

ANCIENT HISTORY

The discovery of cave-drawings of the early Stone-age (see Altamira, tour 3) reveals that Spain was already inhabited about 20,000 years ago. Between 1500 and 500 B.C. Greeks and Phoenicians settled along the Spanish coast. Some Celtic tribes also settled in the peninsula. In the 5th c. the Carthaginians began to colonize Spain and founded Cartagena (New Carthage).

206 B.C. The Romans drove the Carthaginians from Spain.

19 B.C. Under Augustus the Romans completed the conquest of Spain.

A.D. 409–711 The Barbarian invasions began. In 414 the Visigoths crossed the Pyrenees. Toledo became their capital, but in the late 7th c. their power declined.

THE MIDDLE AGES

711 The Moors entered Spain from N. Africa, and reached the Pyrenees by 718. The Christians were able to retain one or two areas, e.g. Asturias and Navarre.

750 Asturias and Cantabria were united under Alfonso I. He later reconquered Galicia, Leon and Old Castile.

756 Conflict arose among the Moorish rulers. One of them broke away and formed an independent *emirate* of Cordoba.

The Moors improved economic conditions and introduced Arabic culture. The Christians of Southern Spain were seldom persecuted, but many of them adopted Moorish customs (the *mozarabs*).

792–842 Alfonso II founded the cathedral of Santiago de Compostela where St James the Apostle was believed to be buried.

912 The Moors introduced artificial irrigation and developed industry.

1002 The Moorish empire in Spain was dissolved into small states.

1027 Ferdinand I became king of Castile, reconquered Galicia and conquered Leon, thus uniting NW. Spain. Rodrigo Diaz de Vivar, 'El Cid' (master), became famous fighting against the Moors.

1086 Toledo was reconquered.

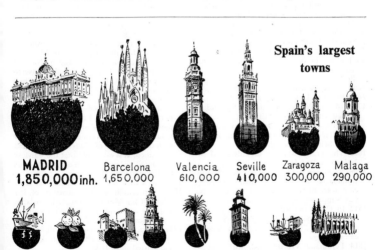

Spain's largest towns

MADRID 1,850,000 inh.

Barcelona 1,650,000

Valencia 610,000

Seville 410,000

Zaragoza 300,000

Malaga 290,000

Bilbao 270,000

Murcia 240,000

Granada 200,000

Cordoba 190,000

Las Palmas 154,000

La Coruña 150,000

Vigo 160,000

Palma de Mallorca 152,000

1236 Cordoba was reconquered, and Seville in 1248.

1263 Alfonso X (1252–84) reconquered Murcia, and Cadiz in 1265.

1462 Under Henry IV (1454–74) Castile captured Gibraltar. After the king's death his sister Isabella succeeded him. She married Ferdinand of Aragon (1479–1516), thus uniting Spain.

MODERN HISTORY

1492 After 11 years of war, Granada, the last Moorish stronghold, was finally conquered. In this year Columbus set out for America. As a result of his expedition and those of men like Cortes and Pizarro, Spain won many territories in the New World.

1516 Charles V (grandson of the Emperor Maximilian and of Ferdinand and Isabella), having inherited the Netherlands in 1506, inherited Spain, and in 1519 also became Holy Roman Emperor.

1556–98 Philip II succeeded Charles in Spain. The protestant Netherlands broke away from Spanish dominion.

1580 Philip II annexed Portugal.

1588 Philip unsuccessfully attempted to invade England with the 'Invincible Armada'. The English replied with attacks on the Spanish treasure-ships returning from America and upon Cadiz and Corunna.

1598 Death of Philip II. Under Philip III Spanish power declined.

1609 12-year armistice with Holland.

1621 Philip IV became king. War broke out again in Holland.

1640 Portugal revolted.

1648 Spain recognized Dutch independence.

1668 Peace of Lisbon with Portugal.

1701–14 The War of the Spanish Succession caused a temporary partition of the country. Her European possessions were lost, Gibraltar and Minorca taken by the British.

1779–83 Minorca reconquered.

1805 The Franco-Spanish fleet defeated by Nelson at Trafalgar.

1808 Napoleon installed his brother, Joseph Bonaparte, as king of Spain, causing civil war. Britain supported the patriots, but Napoleon took Madrid in 1808.

1812 In Cadiz the national parliament, the 'Cortes', signed the first liberal Spanish constitution. Spain lost her South American colonies.

1814 Ferdinand VII returned, with Napoleon's sanction. He suspended the constitution of 1812. This caused a revolution in

1820. The king was forced to recognize the constitution, and two-thirds of the church's property was confiscated.

1843 Strife over the constitution once more arose, culminating in the revolution of 1868.

1875 After various Republican Governments and the brief rule of Italian King Amadeo, Isabella's son Alfonso XII became king, succeeded by his son Alfonso XIII in 1885.

1895 A revolt in Cuba resulted in the Spanish-American war of 1898, as the result of which Spain lost Cuba, Puerto Rico and the Philippines.

1914 Spain was neutral during World War I.

1923 General Primo de Rivera in agreement with the king carried out a coup which made him military dictator.

1931 Municipal elections resulted in a victory for the Republicans, the king voluntarily left for Italy, the Republic was declared, a new constitution was passed.

1936 In May President Zamora was forced to resign. In July a military revolt broke out in Morocco under General Franco. This was the signal for disturbances throughout Spain followed by Civil War. A coalition government was formed, called the 'People's Front'. Supported by part of the navy and air force, and the Catalonian government, it confiscated the church's property and armed the workers of Madrid. With the support of Morocco, Andalusia, Old Castile, Aragon, Navarre and Mallorca, Franco formed a government in Burgos. Formally neither side had support from abroad, but in actual fact Italy and Germany supported Franco, while Russia, France and Mexico supported the 'People's Front'. Support was partly in the form of arms, and partly of volunteers. The war ended in March 1939 with the surrender of Madrid and Valencia to Franco. It is estimated that the war-loss amounted to over a million deaths plus terrible material destruction.

1939 Spain took no part in World War II.

1947 A plebiscite on the question of the return of the Monarchy resulted in a large majority in favour of Franco's continuation as leader of the State.

1949 Some countries re-opened diplomatic relations with Spain after the break which had existed since 1936.

1956 Spain was admitted to full membership of the United Nations.

ART AND ARCHITECTURE

Apart from the prehistoric cave-drawings and a few scattered works, it was not until the late Middle Ages that Spanish art really began to develop. By the 16th century there were three main schools: the *Valencian School* (including Catalonia and Aragon), the *Sevillian School* (Andalusia) and the *Madrid School* (Castile).

VALENCIAN SCHOOL

Francisco Ribalta (1551–1628) was one of the first great Spanish masters. His colours are vivid and there are brilliant contrasts of light and shade. Perhaps you will also see some of the work of his son, *Juan Ribalta*, who specialized mainly in portrait-painting.

José Ribera, called *el Espanoleto* (1568–1656), became Ribalta's greatest pupil. As a young man he went to Naples, where he remained the rest of his life. His pictures have great dramatic effect and there is a masterly use of light and shadow.

SEVILLIAN SCHOOL

Francisco Herrera (1576–1656) was the originator of the Sevillian school.

Francisco Zurbaran (1598–1664), the pupil of Herrera and Ribera, painted portraits, 'still life' and chiefly religious pictures, especially with themes from old legends.

Diego Velasquez (1599–1660) is the most celebrated representative of this school. Although bound to the Italian tradition, he was able to bring to his works some of the Spanish temperament. His paintings are marked by their elegance. He became Chief Court Painter as the result of the first of his portraits of *Philip IV*. He reproduces nature with strict realism and his paintings, chiefly portraits and court scenes or historical and mythological compositions, are characterized by their intense objectivity. Two of his best known pictures are 'The Surrender of Breda' and 'Las Meninas' (The Maids of Honour); both in the Prado at Madrid.

Bartolomé Esteban Murillo (1617–1682) became one of the most popular painters of Seville and his influence on Sevillian art lasted long. He is primarily an Andalusian; this is clearly seen in his religious and mythological paintings in his choice of colour and his depiction of character. Some of his paintings are to be found in Seville (in the museum and Hospital de la Caridad) and many are in the Prado.

MADRID SCHOOL

El Greco is the Spanish name for the Cretan, *Domenikos Theotokopoulos* (1541–1614). As a young man he became the pupil of *Titian* in Venice and was also influenced by *Tintoretto*. In 1577 he settled in Toledo where his home soon became the town's artistic and intellectual centre. One of his most celebrated paintings is the 'Burial of Count Orgaz' (San Tome in Toledo).

Francisco Goya (1746–1828) was an outstanding genius with many varied talents. He created frescoes, etchings, tapestries and paintings with equal virtuosity, and in 1799 became *Charles IV's* court painter. He is not least famous for his satirical etchings. Some of his best paintings are to be found in the Prado, e.g. 'Maja Desnuda' and the famous 'Executions of Moncloa'. The latter, as also the series of etchings, 'Los desastres de la Guerra', expresses the artist's deep-felt disgust for the horrors of war.

The next great Spanish painter and sculptor is *Pablo Picasso*, born in 1881 and still active. His work has stimulated much discussion. After his youthful naturalism (the 'blue' and 'pink' periods), he turned to abstract painting and was one of the creators of cubism. His work is spread over most of the globe and many of his pictures, sculptures and ceramic creations are in private ownership.

Velazquez' famous picture, 'Las Meninas'

The development of architecture in Spain has been very interesting, and on travelling round the country, one is impressed again and again by the many beautiful buildings. Here is a brief introduction to the various periods of architecture.

ROMAN. In Spain, as in other places, the Romans were skilful builders and the ruins of some impressive buildings can still be seen in *Merida* (amphitheatre, aqueduct), *Segovia* (huge aqueduct) and in *Tarragona* (the town wall), as well as in many other places.

MOORISH. The Moors left behind some beautiful and interesting buildings, and also influenced subsequent Spanish architecture. The Mosque in *Cordoba* and the Alhambra in *Granada* are the most notable.

ROMANESQUE. This style reached Spain in the 10th c. Its finest examples can be seen in the cathedral of *Santiago de Compostela* and in Avila and Segovia. (In Portugal: *Coimbra* cathedral and the Knights Templar church in *Tomar*.)

GOTHIC. This style came to Spain from France and is richly represented. The cathedrals of *Barcelona, Burgos, Toledo, Salamanca, Tarragona* and *Palma de Mallorca* are some of the main works of this period.

RENAISSANCE. This age transformed the Gothic tradition but did not entirely discard it at first. Buildings were decorated in the so-called 'plateresque' style (Casa de Pilatos in *Seville*, Colegio de Santa Cruz in *Valladolid* and others). The first fully Renaissance building was Charles V's palace in the Alhambra (*Granada*). Other examples are the cathedral in *Granada* and the façade of the university of *Salamanca. El Escorial* represents a transition to a more severe classicism. But soon afterwards the desire for decoration was revived and led to a 'mixed style' of Plateresque and Baroque (Cartuja-monastery in *Granada*). At the same time the purer Classical style continued, e.g. the Royal Palace in *Madrid*.

NEO-CLASSICISM. The most important building in this style is the Prado in *Madrid*.

ART NOUVEAU. The fantastic church of the Sagrada Familia by Guardi, in *Barcelona*, is a unique example of this style.

National Festivals and Recreations

When in Spain between March and October it is nearly always possible to attend a festival. The Spaniards love celebrating and use every opportunity for doing so.

On religious holidays in all large towns there are colourful processions through the streets to the church, and you will occasionally come across a group of pilgrims.

In Holy Week, *Semana Santa*, the processions are on an especially large scale. If you are to spend Easter in Spain, you should arrange to be in *Seville, Malaga* or *Granada* for the celebrations, where they are particularly magnificent. The tourist should note that during Holy Week and *Ferias* hotels are allowed to double their prices and often demand payment for seven days, even if you stay a shorter time.

BULL-FIGHTING

in its present form dates from the early 18th c. and is still Spain's most popular entertainment, although football is competing with it nowadays. Even if you don't sympathize with bull-fighting, you must visit the arena at least once, to see what it is all about.

For Spaniards bull-fighting is a passion. Everywhere, in cafés, in trains and on the streets you will see Spaniards talking about the latest bull-fights. They express themselves with eloquent gestures illustrating passes of the matador, which will leave you in no doubt as to what the conversation is about.

Tickets for an ordinary *corrida* cost between 50 and 100 pts, though at important fights ringside seats may cost as much as 500 pts. The cheapest places are in the sun (sol), the dearest in the shade (sombra). It is advisable to choose seats in the shade; they are the most comfortable and the matador is often inclined to draw the main fight to that side of the arena, where the sun hinders him least. Arrive early, there is generally a crowd and it usually begins on time. Even if you have to wait a little for the fight to begin, it is impossible to be bored.

The pageant begins when the *presidente*, a paid expert who decides on the timing of each phase of the fight, has arrived. After a fanfare, comes the opening procession: first one or two men on horseback, dressed in 18th-c. costumes. They salute the president. Then follow the *matadors* with their *banderilleros* and *picadors*. The procession ends with a team of mules, used to drag the dead bull out of the arena. All the principals are dressed in fine gold- or silver-embroidered uniforms. The matadors are, of course, the smartest. They remain behind in the arena with their *cuadrillas* of helpers.

The president performs a symbolic presentation of the key to the bull-enclosure, the first bull is let out and the fight begins.

It falls into three parts: firstly, the preparatory rousing of the bull, in which the banderilleros and the matador attempt to tire and mentally 'fix' it. This ends after the picadors from their armoured horses have pierced the bull with their lances.

Next follows the placing of the banderillas by the banderilleros close together in the nape of the bull's neck. They use two weapons at a time, and the action must be graceful and accurate to win the approval of the audience which is very critical. Very rarely loaded banderillas are used on a cowardly bull, which bang and splutter to encourage the animal to attack.

Then follows the decisive part, where the

The first banderillas placed in the bull's neck

matador must show his worth. He dedicates the bull to the president, the public, or some important person, sometimes a lady; he takes off his hat, which he does not put on again until he has killed the bull; and then he begins his dangerous art.

With his red cloak he attracts the bull's attention and provokes it to charge, foiling its attack again and again, by drawing it off to one side with the cloak. He moves with the grace of a dancer, and the closer he is to the bull, the slighter his movements are to avoid its rush, the greater is the applause of the crowd. After a particularly skilful pass the orchestra strikes up a march. When he judges that the moment has come he makes the fatal thrust. The sword has to strike a bit of the nape of the neck about the size of a half-crown, if it is to plunge right in up to the hilt, piercing the heart or lung, and kill the bull at once. If the matador achieves this feat with one swift, clean stroke the applause is endless, but if his first stroke is unsuccessful, he makes another attempt, or if the bull does not die immediately, one of the banderilleros severs the spinal cord with a dagger.

There are usually 6 fights at a performance. Perhaps you will want to leave after one or two, but more probably you will be infected by the terrific enthusiasm of the audience and forget the more gruesome aspect of bull-fighting—in any case you will have seen a unique part of the national life of Spain.

The Language

A LITTLE ABOUT THE PRONUNCIATION.

The Stress is laid on the *penultimate* syllable of a word that ends in a vowel (Gra-*na*da), in a double vowel (ser*vi*cio), in *n* (e*xa*men) and *s* (Valde*pe*nas); on the last syllable of a word ending in a consonant, other than *n* and *s* (Ma*drid*).

The stress which deviates from these rules is indicated by an accent: á, ó, ú etc. (Cór-doba, Bailén, Alcázar). It is important to remember the correct accentuation, as words occasionally have different meanings indicated by the accent.

Vowels are short and open: a as in 'car'; e as the a in 'paper'; i as in 'machine'; o as in 'soft' (in an unstressed open syllable as in 'rope'); u as in 'bull'.

Consonants are a little more difficult. Those especially different from English are: b with a sound halfway between *b* and *v* (Valencia, Avila, Habana); c before *a, o, u* and before a consonant as *k*, before *e* and *i* as *th* in 'think' (Córdoba, Cruz-Cervantes); d is pronounced hard at the beginning of a syllable, before *r* or after *l, n, r, s*; after a vowel *d* is soft (Dinamarca-Madrid, the final *d* is almost inaudible); g is pronounced almost as *ch* in German 'ich', before *e* or *i*; h is not pronounced; j much the same sound as *g* but almost as *h*; ll as *ly* (Sevilla); ñ as 'ny' (señorita); qu as *k* (Quijote), only used before *i* and *e*; r always rolled, as the German tongue-tip *r*; s is always a little lisping (Santiago); z always like *c* before *e* or *i* (see above); v as *b* (see above).

Some Useful Spanish Words

MOTORISTS

Motor-car: *el auto, el coche*
Driver's licence: *el carnet de conductor*
Motor-coach: *el autobus*
Petrol: *la gasolina*
Petrol-tank: *el deposito de gasolina*
Oil: *el aceite*
Motor-cycle: *la motocicleta*
Puncture: *un pinchazo*
Car park: *el aparcamiento para coches*
Water: *agua*
Jack: *el gato*

THE RAILWAY

Station: *la estacion*
Ticket: *billete*
Time-table: *el horario*
Seat: *el asiento*
Train: *el tren*
Dining-car: *el coche-restaurante*
Sleeping-car: *el coche-cama*
Cloakroom: *la consigna*
Porter: *el mozo*
Express-train: *el 'Rapido'*
Tram: *el tranvia*
Waiting room: *la sala de espera*
Information office: *Oficina de informacion*

BOARD AND LODGING

Hotel: *el hotel*
Boarding house: *la pension*
Youth Hostel: *el albergue juvenil*
Camping place: *el camping*
Room: *la habitacion*
Double room: *una habitacion con dos camas* (with two beds), *matrimonio* (with one large bed)
— with bath: *con bano*
Full board: *pension completa*
'Half' board: *media pension*
Ladies' toilet: *el vater de señoras*
Waiter: *el camarero*
Chamber-maid: *la camarera*
Breakfast: *el desayuno*
Meal: *la comida*

Lunch: *el almuerzo*
Dinner: *la cena*
Dining-room: *el comedor*
Menu: *la carte, la lista*
Wine: *el vino* (white: *blanco*, red: *tinto*)
Mineral water: *agua mineral*
A glass: *un vaso*
Wine-glass: *una copa*
Soda water: *sifon*
Coffee: *cafe*. Tea: *te*
The bill: *la cuenta*

SHOPPING

Street: *la calle*
Shop: *la tienda*
Baker: *la panaderia* (for bread, otherwise: *pasteleria*)
Diary: *la mantequeria* (for butter, eggs, etc.) *lecheria* (for milk)
Greengrocer: *la fruteria*
Tobacconist: *el estanco*
Tailor: *el sastre*
Book-shop: *la libreria*
Doctor: *el medico*
Dentist: *el dentisto*
Bank: *el banco*
Yes, no,: *si, no*
You (addressing someone): *Usted* (shortened *Vd.*), plural: *Ustedes* (*Vds.*)
Please: *Sirvase por favor*
May I ask you: *Hagame Usted el favor*
Excuse me, sorry: *Dispenseme Usted, Perdonerne*
Allow me, excuse me: *Con Permiso*
Many thanks: *Muchas gracias*
How much does it cost?: *Cuanto cuesta?*
Altogether: *todo incluido*
It's too dear: *es demasiado caro*
Where is—?: *donde esta—?*

THE TIME

Today: *hoy*. Tomorrow: *mañana*. The day after tomorrow: *pasado mañana*
Yesterday: *ayer*

Midday: *el mediodia*
Afternoon: *la tarde*
Evening: *la noche*
Midnight: *la medianoche*
An hour: *una hora*
Half an hour: *media hora*
A quarter of an hour: *un cuarto de hora*
A minute: *un minuto*
Days of the week: *domingo, lunes, martes, miercoles, jueves, viernes, sabado*
Week: *la semana*. Day: *el dia*
Month: *el mes*. Year: *el ano*
What is the time?: *Que hora es?*

NUMBERS

1 *uno, una*; 2 *dos*; 3 *tres*; 4 *cuatro*; 5 *cinco*; 6 *seis*; 7 *siete*; 8 *ocho*; 9 *nueve*; 10 *diez*; 11 *once*; 12 *doce*; 13 *trece*; 14 *catorce*; 15 *quince*; 16 *dieciseis*; 17 *diecisiete*; 18 *dieciocho*; 19 *diecinueve*; 20 *veinte*; 21 *veintiuno*; 22 *veintidos*; 23 *veintitres*. etc. 30 *treinta*; 31 *treinta y uno*; 32 *treinta y dos* etc.; 40 *cuarenta*; 50 *cincuenta*; 60 *sesenta*; 70 *setenta*; 80 *ochenta*; 90 *noventa*; 100 *ciento* (in daily use before nouns: *cien*, e.g. *cien pesetas*); 101 *ciento uno*; 110 *ciento diez*; 200 *doscientos* (fem. *doscientas*); 300 *trescientos*; 400 *cuatrocientos*; 500 *quinientos*; 600 *seiscientos*; 700 *setecientos*; 800 *ochocientos*; 900 *novecientos*; 1000 *mil*; 2000 *dos mil*; 1 million *un millon*; 1st, 2nd, 3rd, 4th, etc.: *el primero, segundo, tercero, cuarto, quinto, sexto, septimo, octavo, noveno, decimo* (fem. *la primera, segunda, etc.*). In dates ordinal numbers are used only for the first; e.g. 1° *de abril*, but 2 *de mayo*.

PREPARING FOR THE TRIP

WHEN TO GO

Avoid July and August, especially if you intend to stay in Central or Southern Spain. Even Spaniards find these months too hot; in fact the government moves from *Madrid* to *San Sebastian* on July 19th. Spring is the best time, from mid-March until the beginning of June, but autumn, from 15th Sept. to mid-Nov., is also suitable. In the winter months it is very pleasant on the coast between Algeciras and Alicante.

PASSPORT AND VISA

For a passport, apply to the nearest Ministry of Labour Employment Exchange, or one of the main Passport Offices: Clive House, Petty France, London, S.W.1; India Buildings, Water Street, Liverpool 2; 14, Princes Square, 48 Buchanan Street, Glasgow, C.2. Two passport photographs are needed (between $2 \times 1\frac{1}{2}$ in. and $2\frac{1}{2} \times 2$ in.). A new passport costs 30s., five years' renewal 20s., and a yearly renewal 4s.

Visas are *not* necessary for entry into Spain for a visit of less than three months. They can be obtained from the Spanish Embassy (Consular Section), 3 Hans Crescent, London, S.W.1.

MOTORISTS

Can get the necessary Customs documents (International Carnet) in advance from the AA or RAC. Motor vehicles should bear the International Registration letters GB. International Vehicle and Driving Permits are still needed in Spain and Portugal. Don't forget to get an International 'Green Card' from your insurance company.

CURRENCY

Travel allowance in foreign currency or travellers' cheques is no longer restricted, but for amounts in excess of £250 per year (1st Nov. to 31st Oct.) an application has to be made to the Bank of England. Passports still have to be marked. An additional £50 in sterling is allowed for use in transit.

The unit of coinage in Spain is the *Peseta* (abbreviated to *Pta.*, plural *Pts.* or *Ptas.*), which is divided into 100 *Centimos* (*Cts.*). At the present rate of exchange 168 pts. are equivalent to £1. 1 pta. is approximately $1\frac{1}{2}d$. Banknotes in circulation are to the value of 1, 5, 25, 100, 500 and 1000 pts. and coins to the value of 1, 2, 2.50 and 50 pts. and 5, 10 and 50 cts.

There is no limit to the amount of foreign currency and travellers' cheques which visitors may take into Spain and up to 50,000 pts. may be brought in in cash. Up to 3000 pts. may be taken out as well as any foreign currency which has not been exchanged in Spain. Don't forget that foreign coins of small denominations will not be accepted by British banks.

CUSTOMS REGULATIONS

On the outward journey: You may take, duty-free, foodstuffs for your own use and personal equipment, which may include such items as a bicycle, camera, typewriter, gramophone, wireless, 250 gr.(9 oz.) of tobacco, 200 cigarettes or 50 cigars, and sporting or camping equipment.

On returning home: Up to 25,000 pts. worth of Spanish goods may be taken out of Spain without an export licence. You must declare any purchases made while abroad, but the following are usually allowed in duty free: 200 gr. of tobacco (see above), $\frac{1}{2}$ bottle of spirits—brandy, whisky, gin, liqueurs, etc.—and 1 bottle of wine.

EQUIPMENT

Only a light wardrobe is needed for nine months of the year. However, the Spaniards are not so free as we are in the matter of dress. Men do not go into the street without a jacket. Women must be particularly careful, and must cover their heads and shoulders when going into a church. Neither men nor women may wear shorts in the street. Ladies' two-piece bathing costumes are actually forbidden by law though the law is now only enforced on city beaches. Men may wear bathing shorts but not trunks, except on non-city beaches.

TIPS

It is sensible always to have some small change in your pocket when you go out. One often needs to give a small tip: to guides on coach-tours, to drivers, museum guides, ushers or usherettes in theatre or cinema. Hotels and restaurants normally add 15% for service to the bill, but waiters, porters and chambermaids often expect a little extra.

How to get to Spain

By Rail, Road, Sea and Air

BY RAIL: Wherever you are going to eventually in Spain you have to go through *Paris* and from here there are two routes, both from the *Gare Austerlitz*, (1) via *Bordeaux–Irun–San Sebastian–Valladolid* to *Madrid*, (2) via *Toulouse–Port Bou–Gerona* to *Barcelona*. On both there are nightly services throughout the year, (1) leaving *Paris* 10.40 p.m. arriving *Madrid* 8.30 p.m. (or 8.40 a.m., 'Talgo Express' from *Irun* on Mon., Wed., Fri. & Sun., 1st cl. only plus supplement), (2) leaving *Paris* 9 p.m. arriving *Barcelona* 1.50 p.m. On both routes there are sleepers, couchettes and dining-cars. There are connections, (1) from *San Sebastian* to *Bilbao–Santander* and from *Valladolid* to *Leon–La Coruña*, (2) from *Gerona* to the *Costa Brava*; otherwise you continue, (1) from *Madrid* to *Lisbon* or *Andalusia*, (2) from *Barcelona* to *Valencia–Alicante* or the *Balearic Isles* (by boat or air).

NB—as the gauge is wider in Spain, you will have to change trains at the frontiers.

BY ROAD: From *London* it takes about 3 days by car to *Barcelona* or *San Sebastian* and 4 to *Madrid*, and about 2 more to the furthest parts of the peninsular, e.g. *Lisbon* or *Cadiz*. But you can save time by taking the night-ferry from *Southampton* to *Le Havre* or by using one of the many air-ferry services run by SILVER CITY AIRWAYS. The map shows the main routes, but the AA or RAC will issue detailed route-cards and also book ferry passages for you. If you have time to dawdle through France, you could use an excellent small book called *Little Roads to Spain.*

Motor Coaches: EUROPABUS runs coach services from London to Barcelona via Brussels leaving on Fridays and Saturdays at 7.15 a.m. and arriving Mondays and Tuesdays at 6.45 p.m. The return fare inclusive of hotels and meals is about the same as the 1st class rail return.

BY SEA: There are a few sailings a month from *London* or *Southampton* to *Vigo, Lisbon* or *Gibraltar*, or from *Liverpool* to *Oporto*.

BY AIR: There are frequent direct services from *London* to *Madrid, Barcelona* and *Palma* by both BEA and IBERIA AIR LINES, and from *Manchester* to *Barcelona* and *Palma* by BEA. All these flights take approx. $3\frac{1}{2}$ hrs. BEA also run regular services from *London* to *Gibraltar* ($4\frac{1}{2}$ hrs) and a direct tourist night-flight to *Valencia* ($3\frac{1}{2}$ hrs). There are also frequent connections by IBERIA from *Madrid* and *Barcelona* to *Seville, Malaga, Vigo, Santiago, Valencia* and *Palma*.

INFORMATION can be obtained from the SPANISH STATE TOURIST OFFICE, 70 Jermyn Street, London, S.W.1.

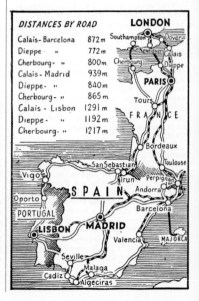

DISTANCES BY ROAD		
Calais–Barcelona	872 m
Dieppe– "	772 m
Cherbourg– "	800 m
Calais–Madrid	939 m
Dieppe– "	840 m
Cherbourg– "	865 m
Calais–Lisbon	1291 m
Dieppe– "	1192 m
Cherbourg– "	1217 m

What is the Fare ?

The fares given below are based on the lists in force in July 1962; but they are all subject to alteration and are only intended as a guide. Rail singles are half the return fares. The rail fares include the Channel crossings. The ones given are for routes via *Dunkirk*, *Calais* or *Boulogne*; for routes via *Dieppe* or *Le Havre* the fares come to about £1 cheaper. Beyond the Franco-Spanish frontier it is possible to travel 3rd class, which can reduce the fare by several pounds. There are a number of different ways of getting from London to Paris, including SKYWAYS' coach–air–coach services, which are quick, comfortable and cheap. For further details see *Gateway Guide to Paris* or consult your nearest travel agency.

London to	Railway Returns		Air		
	1st Cl.	2nd Cl.	Single	Return	Tourist Return*
	£ s. d.	£ s. d.	£ s. d.	£ s. d.	£ s. d.
Algeciras	45 14 0	32 2 0	—	—	—
Barcelona	34 8 0	23 12 0	23 18 0	43 1 0	32 12 0
Granada	42 16 0	29 18 0	—	—	—
Madrid	37 0 0	25 14 0	29 7 0	52 17 0	36 15 0
Malaga	44 10 0	31 2 0	33 13 0	60 12 0	47 2 0
San Sebastian	29 14 0	20 6 0	—	—	—
Seville	43 16 0	30 12 0	34 13 0	62 8 0	46 6 0
Tarragona	35 10 0	24 8 0	—	—	—
Valencia	38 14 0	26 4 0	26 13 0	48 0 0	35 5 0
Gibraltar	*see Algeciras*		29 7 0	52 17 0	37 15 0
Palma	—	—	26 1 0	46 18 0	36 10 0
Manchester to					
Barcelona	41 6 0	28 4 0	25 16 0	46 9 0	35 9 0
Palma	—	—	27 19 0	50 7 0	39 7 0

* These night-flights are slightly cheaper on week-days.

On all main-line trains through France there are *restaurant cars*, in which you can get an excellent lunch or dinner for about 12s. 6d. *Seat reservations* cost 2s. 6d. On night trains to *Irun* and *Port Bou* there are *couchettes* and *sleepers*; it is advisable to book these well in advance. The fares are at present:

Paris to	Irun	Port Bou
	£ s. d.	£ s. d.
Couchettes		
1st and 2nd cl.	1 5 0	1 5 0
Sleepers		
1st cl. single berth	7 4 6	8 10 6
special	4 11 6	5 6 0
double	3 6 6	3 18 0
2nd cl.	2 19 6	3 12 6

Travelling in Spain

The greater width of Spanish **TRAINS** means that the carriages are more spacious, and, as seat reservations are obligatory on all main lines, the trains do not become over-crowded. It is very important to reserve seats in advance, either through one of the offices of the Spanish railway (RENFE) or through a travel agency. Without a reservation it is doubtful whether you will be allowed on the train, nor with a ticket bought at home if it has not been stamped first at the station of departure.

The most comfortable train in Spain is the 'TALGO Express', which runs between *Irun* and *Madrid* (see p. 12). It is an ultra-modern express train with air-conditioning, bar, dining-car and great speed. There is only one class and a supplement is necessary.

TAF-Diesel trains, which run on most main lines, are also modern and fast. On these trains there is also only one class and a supplement.

Sleeping compartments can only be ob-tained by holders of 1st or 2nd class tickets. One can choose between one- and two-bunk compartments—the two-bunk ones are usually 2nd class.

It is particularly advantageous to buy a kilometre ticket (*kilometrico*) which entitles you to travel from 3000 to 12,000 kms. in any train. A 1st class kilometre ticket can be used on the TALGO but one must also pay a supplement. These tickets can be bought within Spain or abroad and they have one further advantage that they can be used by more than one person.

The ticket must have a photograph(s) of the holder(s). The prices given here refer to tickets purchased abroad and include the fee for seat reservation. Under certain regulations tickets can be lengthened, if the number of kilometres for which they are issued are not sufficient.

All main-line trains are provided with dining-cars. Prices of meals are approx.: breakfast—15 pts., lunch and dinner—55 pts., to which must be added 15% for service.

One is allowed free conveyance of up to 30 kg. registered luggage. Porters expect a small tip. Luggage can only be reckoned to be conveyed by these trains on journeys to or from the border. Otherwise it is trans-ported by the previous or the following train

TRAVELLING BY BUS

The Spanish bus company, ATESA, caters for a number of inclusive tours within Spain, i.e. bus journeys plus hotel accommodation and food. The same company as well as travel agencies arrange sight-seeing tours in the large towns. As both the hotels and the restaurants used are of the highest standard, prices are relatively high. Other bus tours within Spain are arranged by private Spanish travel agencies. It is best to make inquiries and reservations through British travel agencies. There are a number of ordinary bus routes between the larger towns. The most important are named after the various tours.

AIR TRAVEL

Travelling by air is relatively cheap in Spain. It is cheaper to buy tickets in Spain and reservations cannot be made abroad.

SEA TRAVEL

There are regular services to the *Balearic Islands* (Palma) from the mainland; from *Barcelona*, *Valencia* and *Alicante*. The fares (singles) are approximately: 1st cl., £2 15s.; 2nd cl., £2 2s.: 3rd cl., £1. From *Palma* to *Ibiza* costs the same.

Staying the Night

HOTELS are grouped into categories, which ensures a more or less uniform standard wherever they may be. Approximate mini-mum prices are as follows; the charges for some rooms may be higher, especially in luxury hotels in July and August. A 15% ser-vice charge must be added to the prices quoted, and a 2% tourist tax to bills of over 100 pts.

Category	Single Room Room	Single Room Full Board	Private Sitting Rooms	Balconies
Luxury (Lujo)	*Pts.* 135	*Pts.* 265	*Pts.* 110	*Pts.* 60
1st cl. A	95	210	65	30
1st cl. B	70	155	40	20
2nd cl.	50	129	25	10
3rd cl.	40	106	10	5

All prices are given in *pesetas*. Most tourists will certainly prefer hotels in class 1A or 1B, in some cases perhaps in class 2. In general 3rd cl. hotels cannot be recommended. They are only included in this book in those places where we could find no 2nd cl. hotel. Our symbols can be interpreted as follows:

🏛🏛 Luxury (always indicated)
    1st cl. A
🏛 1st cl. B
🏛 2nd cl. (occasionally 3rd)

The so-called *Fondas*, found mainly in small towns, are even more simple, with lower prices.

An innovation by the Spanish Tourist Department are the so-called *Paradores*, which have been arranged in some of the most beautiful places in Spain. One often finds a *Parador* in an old castle or monastery. They are furnished with taste and the food is excellent. Their prices are rather above the average for their category of 1A but they are places one will enjoy visiting, either for a meal or to spend the night. In Portugal there are similar hotels called *Pousadas*.

The Tourist Department has also erected inns on main roads outside large towns, the *Albergues de Carretera*; also recommended.

The *Paradores* and the *Albergues de Carretera* are mentioned in the various tours, when a break for lunch or a night's rest seemed called for, but occasionally they are also mentioned, because they are particularly worth stopping at.

YOUTH HOSTELS

The Spanish Youth Hostel Association is very new; there is a small but growing number of hostels, which are open to all members of the Youth Hostel Association. Details of them are given in an annual catalogue issued by: *Red Española de Albergues Juveniles* (R.E.A.J.), José Ortega y Gasset 71, Madrid. International membership cards (120 pts.) are obtainable from this address but it is more convenient to join your own association in advance (Y.H.A., Trevelyan House, St Albans, Herts; Y.H.A. of Scotland, 7 Bruntsfield Crescent, Edinburgh).

To spend a night in a hostel costs 16 pts. Breakfast costs 6–10 pts., lunch and supper each cost 20 pts. Payment for meals and lodging must be made on arrival. In July and August it is necessary to reserve accommodation in advance. Further details and special advance booking postcards, which cost 2*d.* each, can be obtained by sending a stamped addressed envelope (4*d.* postage for a dozen cards) to Y.H.A. Travel, 29 John Adam Street, London, W.C.2.

CAMPING

The camping movement is also comparatively new in Spain, but in recent years some camping places have been opened, authorized by the *Comite Español de Camping*, Via Layetana 30, Barcelona. Some of these places are included in the tours. There are, however, possibilities for pitching camp in other places, although there may be a shortage of water in Central Spain and it would be sensible to take a supply from the last town. If there are police nearby, it would be wise to ask for permission.

What to Eat and what it Costs

Meals in Spain are certainly very different from those you are used to at home. But when you have become accustomed to meals prepared in oil and the use of garlic in many dishes, you will find that the food is really excellent. So don't give up straight away.

In 1962 the price on standard menus in Spanish hotels is as follows:

Class	Breakfast	Main Meal
Luxury	30	80
1st Class A	25	70
1st Class B	22	60
2nd Class	17	50
3rd Class	14	40

To these prices must be added service charges of 15%. There are also often local purchase taxes and wine taxes.

Times of meals are rather late by our standards; lunch is served from 2 p.m. and dinner from 9 p.m. The further South you are, the later you will eat. It is not unusual to eat dinner between 10 and 11 in the evening.

The following may be of help to you in deciphering the Spanish menu (la carta).

Entremeses	**First Course**
Ensalada	Salad, with olives, tomatoes and onions in a dressing of oil and vinegar
Lechuga (lettuce)	Green salad, dressed with oil and vinegar
Jamon, serrano	Ham, smoked and dried
Jamon, dulce	Ham, boiled
Mantequilla	Butter (unsalted)
Esparragos	Asparagus
Tortilla	Omelet
Huevos (poches, fritos, pasados por aque)	Egg (poached, fried, boiled)

Pescado	**Fish**
Merluza	Hake
Calamares	Cuttle-fish
Lenguado	Sole
Caracoles	Snails
Gambas	Prawns
Gambas a la plancha	Grilled hot prawns
Langostinos	Large prawns
Langostas	Crawfish
Almejas	Clams
Ostras	Oysters

Carne	**Meat**
Biftec	Fried veal
Costillo de cordero	Mutton cutlet
Corderito	Lamb
Escalore de ternera	Veal cutlet in breadcrumbs
Higado	Liver

Rinones	Kidneys
Sesos	Brains
Butifarra	Sausage
Salchichas de Francfort	Frankfurters
Pollo (al asta)	Chicken (grilled on a spit)

Macaroni Dishes	
Tallarines	Macaroni
Canalones	Rolled Macaroni, filled with chopped liver

Postres	**Sweets**
Fruta variada	Assorted fruit
Helado	Ice cream
Queso	Cheese
Flan	Crème caramel

WHAT TO DRINK

Avoid drinking ordinary tap water except in Madrid—wine is cheap and normally much healthier. One can choose between white (*vino blanco*) and red wine (*vino tinto*) and there is a wide choice of mineral waters.

You will generally be offered ordinary table wine at meal times (*vino corriente*). Wine from Rioja is the best known, but that from Valdepeñas is also excellent.

It is a usual practice to add water or mineral water to the wine as it has a much higher alcoholic content than French wine.

If you must have water, ask for mineral water, but it is sometimes dearer than wine. You can also obtain orange juice, *naranjada*, and lemonade, *limonada*, not to forget the lovely juice of freshly pressed grapes, *Batido de uvas* (a little dearer).

Sherry is naturally preferred by many as an aperitif; we are after all in its native land. Here are the names of the different types of sherry: *fino*, very dry; *amontillado*, dry; *palo cortado*, medium dry; *oloroso*, medium sweet; *abocado*, sweet. *Dulce* is a very sweet, dark dessert wine and *manzanilla* is a light, dry aperitif, like sherry. Vermouth is also much used as an aperitif. If you like something to nibble at while you enjoy your drink, ask for *tapas* and you will be brought a small saucer with salted almonds, roasted nuts, fresh sardines, olives, roasted cuttle-fish, potato crisps, or any of a dozen different tit-bits.

A sweet and wonderful tasting dessert wine is *Malaga*; a similar wine is produced in *Alicante* and *Tarragona*. There are many good liqueurs, and Spanish brandy, which is much cheaper than French, is excellent.

MADRID

MADRID (about 2000 ft. above sea level, pop. 1,850,000), the capital of Spain, lies almost in the geographical centre of the country. NW of the city are the mountain ranges, *Sierra de Guadarrama* and *Sierra de Gredos*, and towards the S. are the *Toledo mountains*. In the E. and SE. is the plateau '*La Mancha*', the landscape of *Don Quixote* and *Sancho Panza*. Madrid is situated in *Castilla la Nueva* (New Castile) and covers an area of ca. 80 sq. km.

The former Royal Palace, the Palacio Real

The name *Madrid* comes from the arabic '*Magerit*', the name of a fortress, erected by the Moors in A.D. 939. The Christian king, *Alfonso VI*, took the town in 1083, and *Philip II* brought his court here in 1561. After becoming the capital, the town grew. A few old buildings originate from this time, but it was *Charles III*, late in the 18th century, who, above anyone else, left his mark on the city by erecting many of the beautiful buildings still to be seen.

During the Spanish civil war from November 1936 to March 1939 the city was attacked and besieged by the nationalist troops. It suffered great damage, which has since been repaired.

The oldest part of the city stretches from the Royal palace, *Palacio Real*, E. to the *Paseo del Prado*, N. to the *Avenida de Jose Antonio* ('Gran Via') and S. to the outer boulevards, the so-called '*Rondas*'. In the centre of this district are the lively squares, *Plaza Mayor* and *Puerta del Sol*. The latter is dominated by a large yellow building, erected

as a post-office in 1786, with a tower of 1847, now occupied by the police.

A tour through the town

As you will see from the map, the most important places in Madrid can be visited by taking a walk right through the old quarter. Numbers in square brackets refer to the map. Begin at the

Palacio Real [1], formerly the royal palace, which is near the *Estacion del Norte* (N. station). It stands on the *Plaza de Oriente*, one of the town's largest squares, which originates from Napoleon's rule, when a whole quarter of the town was pulled down. On the square are the marble statues of Spanish kings; in the middle is the equestrian statue of Philip IV (1640) designed by Velazquez. The palace, in style partly Renaissance and partly neo-classical, was built between 1738–64, with additions in 1845 (the lower S. wing). In the inner court are statues of the Spanish-born Roman emperors *Trajan, Hadrian, Theodosius* and *Honorius*. There are many beautiful rooms: the throne room, the porcelain room, and the hall of mirrors.

A collection of valuable tapestries, including some from the Emperor Charles V's time, is sometimes open to the public. In one wing there is a weapon museum, *La Armeria Real*, a collection begun by Charles V. The square between the wings is the *Plaza de Armas* and from its W. side there is a magnificent view over the park, which is called the *Campo del Moro* in memory of the Moorish siege of the *Alcazar* (1109). The *Alcazar* stood where the *Plaza de Oriente* is today.

Pass the unfinished church, *Catedral de Nuestra Señora de la Almudena*, going along the *Calle de Bailen* to the viaduct over the *Calle de Segovia*. A little further on to the r. is the church of

San Francisco el Grande [2] (1761–84), which has a beautiful interior, and in the first chapel to the l. is a picture by *Goya*.

Return over the viaduct and turn to the r. along the *Calle Mayor*, which leads to the *Puerta del Sol*. On the r. is the *Plaza de la Villa* with the town hall, *Ayuntamiento* [3], a lovely 17th-c. building. Also in the square are the *Casa de Cisneros*

TOURS
To Escorial, Segovia & Valladolid
To University City

⑤

& ⑰

To Avila,
Salamanca
& Lisbon

CALLE DE ALBERTO AQUILERA

C.DE CARRANZA

C. DE SAGASTA

PL.STA
BARBARA

CALLE DE LA PRINCESA

CALLE DE SAN BERNARDO

CALLE DE FUENCARRAL

CALLE DE HORTALEZA

⑯

PLAZA DE
⑰
ESPAÑA

JERONIMO DOMINGO

AVENIDA DE JOSE ANTONIO

G

Telefónica

ESTACIÓN
DEL NORTE

REDONDO

PASEO ONESIMO

CALLE DE PRECIADOS

CALLE DE MONTERA

D

C.DE CARMEN

F

CALLE DE ALCALÁ

⑱ 600 m

To

Royal
Palace

⑥

Campo
del
Moro

PLAZA
DE
ORIENTE

Theatre

C. DEL ARENAL

PUERTA
DEL SOL

CARRERA DE S.JERONIMO

Cortes
Española

①

Armeria

BAILEN

E H

C.DE CARRETAS

P. DE LAS
CORTES

T B

CALLE MAYOR

PLAZA
MAYOR

C.DEL CARMEN

CALLE DE
SEGOVIA

③

④

CONCEP. JERONIMA

CALLE DE LAS HUERTAS

N7
to Merida &
Lisbon (Portugal)

CALLE DE TOLEDO

PL. TIRSO
DE MOLINA

CALLE DE ATOCHA

②

C. DE S.FRANCISCO

⑤

RIBERA DE CURTIDOR

CALLE DE EMBAJADORES

C. DE ARGUMOSA

RONDA DE SEGOVIA

C. CALATRAVAS

DEL OLIVAR

DE VALENCIA

C. DE ARGUMOSA

PUERTA TOLEDO

RONDA DE TOLEDO

P. GEN. PRIMO D.RIVERA

P. DE LAS ACACIAS

½ km to
ESTACIÓN DE
LAS DELICIAS

N 401 to Toledo

18

MADRID

Showing the main streets.

0 1 2 3 4 500 m

To Burgos & Irun

To ½ km. **A**

TOUR **4**

8

TOUR **13**

To Barcelona

DE GENOVA

PASEO DE LA CASTELLANA

PLAZA DE COLON

CALLE DE SERRANO

CALLE DE GOYA

CALLE DE ALCALA

PASEO DE RECOLETOS

7

CALLE DE AVENIDA MENENDEZ PELAYO

CALLE DE O'DONELL

9

PLAZA DE LA CIBELES

Post Office

Parque del Retiro

CALLE DE IBIZA

10

PL. DE LA LEALTAD

11

XII

12

PL. DE CANOVAS

Entrance

PASEO DEL PRADO

15

Prado museum

CALLE DE ALFONSO

Zoo

13

Jardin Botanico

14

C. DE CLAUDIO MOYANO

C

PLAZA DEL EMPERADOR CARLOS V

ESTACIÓN DEL MEDIODIA

CALLE DE LA CIUDAD DE BARCELONA

N III
to Valencia

TOUR **6**

To Aranjuez & Córdoba

Sights: 1. Palacio Real. 2. San Francisco el Grande. 3. Ayuntamiento. 4. Plaza Mayor. 5. Flea market. 6. Academia de Bellas Artes. 7. Museo de Arte Moderno. 8. Museo Lazaro Galdiano. 9. Puerta de Alcala. 10. Museo de Reproducciones Artísticas 11. Military museum. 12. Retiro Park. 13. Zoo. 14. Botanical Gardens. 15. The Prado. 16. Museo Municipal. 17. Cervantes monument. 18. San Antonio de la Florida.

Hotels: A. Castellana Hilton. B. Palace. C. Nacional. D. Cliper. E. Internacional. F. Regina. G. Continental. H. Ultramar.

State Tourist Office: T.

19

Madrid

and the *Torre de los Lujanes* (both 16th c., later restored). The square is characteristic of 16th–17th-c. Madrid. Continue along the *Calle Mayor* and turn again to the r. at the *Plaza Mayor* [4], which is surrounded by large 17th-c. houses. Tournaments, bullfights, plays, political meetings, and *auto-dafes* used to be held here. In the middle is the equestrian statue of Philip III (1613). Along the *Calle de Toledo* we come to the *Plaza del Rastro*, with Madrid's *flea market* [5] (especially lively on Sunday mornings). Further on is the *Puerta de Toledo* (1827).

Return to the *Plaza Mayor* and walk to the r. along the *Calle Mayor* until you come to the *Puerta del Sol*. Go past the yellow police building and continue along the busy *Calle de Alcala*. On the l. is the art gallery, *Academia de Bellas Artes* [6], which contains some good paintings by Dutch, Italian and Spanish masters (*Goya* and *Zurbaran*). In the *Plaza de la Cibeles* is the huge General Post-Office and next door to it the Ministry of Naval Affairs with an interesting *naval museum*. We now turn to the l. along the *Paseo de Recoletos*. On the r., just before the *Plaza de Colon* with the statue of Columbus (60 ft. high) is the huge *Palacio de la Biblioteca y Museos Nacionales* [7]. There are some interesting collections here: *Museo de Arte Moderno*, a collection of 19th and 20th-c. Spanish art; the *Museo Arqueologico Nacional*, the national archaeological museum; also an 'American Museum', containing ethnographical collections from Central and Southern America. This collection is later to be moved to the *University City*. The block also houses the large *National Library*, including 800 different editions of *Don Quixote*, numerous old manuscripts, a book collection of over a million volumes and over 100,000 engravings and wood-cuts.

At No. 112 *Calle de Serrano* is the largest private art collection in Spain, the *Museo Lazaro Galdiano* [8], which now belongs to the state. Besides a large collection of English paintings, porcelain and ceramic collections, and numerous paintings by famous Dutch and Italian masters, the great Spanish painters are also well represented.

Along the *Calle de Serrano* we come to the *Plaza de Independencia* with *Puerta de Alcala* [9], an arch from the old city walls built as it stands today in 1778. From this square one can enter the famous *Retiro park* (see below). We walk beside the park along the *Avenida*

de Alfonso XII. At No. 28 is the *Museo de Reproducciones Artisticas* [10], a collection of plaster casts and other copies of famous works of art. Behind lies the *Military Museum* [11], *Museo del Ejercito*, with a collection of military equipment from different epochs. Now returning along the Avenida de Alfonso XII, we turn to the r. and stand at the main entrance to the *Retiro Park* [12], which was laid out by Philip II. It stretches over a huge area (350 acres). The entrance is very stately and opens on to an alley, leading to a lake, *El Estanque Grande*. The park is laid out with fountains, sculptures, temples, colonnades and there are two buildings for exhibitions. The loveliest part is in the SE corner. Here is *Madrid's Zoo* [13]. We now return to the *botanical gardens* [14]. Along the *Calle de Claudio Moyano*—skirting the gardens—we come to the square, *Glorieta de Atocha*, with the Southern station, *Estacion de Mediodia*. Going down the *Paseo del Prado*, we come to the impressive *Museo del Prado* [15], which contains one of the world's most famous collections of paintings. It would take days or weeks to go through the gallery thoroughly—there are over 2500 paintings—but even a hasty visit is worth while. It is preferable to go in the morning, when the lighting is best, and it is easiest to use the side-entrance and go straight up to the first floor. Of the Italian masters, pay special attention to Raphael's *The Cardinal*, Fra Angelico's *The Anunciation*, a copy of Leonardo da Vinci's *Mona Lisa*, and *Christ reveals himself to Mary Magdalene* by Correggio, Veronese's *Venus and Adonis*, and Titian's *Charles V at Augsburg*.

The main entrance to the Prado

Paintings by Tintoretto include *The woman with the bared breast* and *Jesus washes the apostles' feet*. Following this see the works of the three great Spaniards, El Greco, Velazquez and Goya. The paintings of El Greco, include *Cavalier with his hand on his breast*, *The Crucifixion*, *The Trinity*, and *The Resurrection*; by Velazquez you can see *The Adoration of the Magi*, *Christ on the cross*, *Los Borrachos* (the tipplers), *Vulcan's Forge*, *Las Lanzas* (The Surrender of Breda), the famous *Las Meninas*, and many portraits.

Among the works of Goya are the famous execution picture *The 3rd of May 1808*, *Charles IV's family* and the two paintings, *La Maja desnuda* and *La Maja vestida* (the dressed and the naked 'Maja'). Naturally other Spanish artists are also represented, e.g. Murillo, Zurbaran, Ribera, Ribalta.

Continue now along the *Paseo del Prado* to the *Plaza de Canovas del Castillo* with the *Fuente de Neptuno* (18th c.). Here are some of Madrid's leading luxury hotels. This square merges into the *Plaza de Lealtad* with the monument of liberation, *Dos de Mayo* (2nd of May), in memory of the Spaniards who fell during the revolt against the French, in 1808. The *Paseo de Prado* continues to the *Plaza de la Cibeles*, but we return to the *Plaza Canovas* and turn into the *Plaza de las Cortes* with the parliament building (*Cortes Españolas*). We go on along the *Carrera de San Jeronimo* to the *Puerta del Sol*. Here we can either end our tour, or we can finish it off with a few more sights.

From the *Puerta del Sol* walk along the busy *Calle de la Montera* to the *Avenida de Jose Antonio*, known as 'Gran Via'. The skyscraper on the corner of *Calle de Fuencarral* is the main telephone exchange (16 storeys). At No. 78 *Calle de Fuencarral* is the *Museo Municipal* [16], Madrid's municipal museum. Return to the 'Gran Via' and turn to the r. until you come to the *Plaza de España*, where you see the modern 37-storey skyscraper hotel, 'Plaza'. On the square stands the *Cervantes monument* [17] representing Don Quixote and his faithful Sancho Panza. From here one can go on to the modern university town, or visit *San Antonio de la Florida* [18]. There are some beautiful frescoes in the dome by Goya, who is buried here.

Looking from the main post-office over the Plaza de la Cibeles towards the city centre

🚂 From *Estacion del Norte* to Bilbao, La Coruña, Irun, Salamanca, Santiago, Santander, Oporto.

From *Estacion de las Delicias* to Lisbon.

From *Estacion del Mediodia* to Algeciras, Alicante, Almeria, Aranjuez, Barcelona, Cadiz, Cordoba, Granada, Jerez de la Frontera, Malaga, Murcia, Seville, Toledo Valencia, Zaragoza.

🚌 To Alicante and Valencia (from *Paseo Reina Christina* 26); to Escorial, San Sebastian and Santander (from *Alenza* 20); to Aranjuez (from *Paseo de Santa Maria de la Cabeza* 11); to Toledo.

✈ To Barcelona, Palma, Valencia, Seville, Malaga, Santiago de Compostila, Bilbao, San Sebastian.

🏨 [A] Castellana Hilton, Paseo Castellana 55. [B] Palace, Plaza de las Cortes 7 (both L.). [C] Nacional, Paseo del Prado 54. [D] Cliper, Chinchilla 6. 🏨 [E] Internacional, Arenal 19. [F] Regina, Alcala 19. 🏨 [G] Continental, and Valencia, Avenida de Jose Antonio 44. [H] Ultramar, Arenal 15, and Alicante, Arenal 16.

▲ Albergue Ruiz de Alda, Avenida de la Habana 139 (4 km from the centre).

△ Near *Puerta de Hierro* on the road to *Escorial*.

State Tourist Office: Dugue Medinaceli 2.
British Consulate: Fernando el Santo 16.

BARCELONA

BARCELONA (pop. 1,650,000), the second largest city in Spain and the most important centre of industry and business, is low-lying, sheltered by the hills of *Tibidabo* and *Mont-Juich*. Its harbour is one of the largest in the Mediterranean.

The interesting old quarter, by the harbour, stretches to the ring roads ('*rondas*'), which are laid on the site of the old town wall. Here the streets are narrow and irregular, in contrast to the newer part of the town, which is notable for the quadratic lay-out of its streets.

Founded in pre-historic times, it was later taken over by the Romans, the Visigoths, and subsequently by the Moors.

It is a lively city with a Southern character. From the town it is possible to go on a number of interesting excursions. The *Ramblas*, which stretch from the *Plaza de Cataluña* to the harbour and divide the old quarter into two is a good place to visit, to see something of the national character of the people. Below we describe a tour of the town, for which, however, you will need a few days, if you are really to enjoy it.

A view over part of the harbour with the Columbus Monument

Tour of the town. The numbers in square brackets refer to the map.

The *Plaza de Cataluña* [1] is Barcelona's largest square with much traffic, which is directed around a garden and several fountains. The colossal building on the Eastern edge of the square is the telephone exchange. Sit a while in a street-cafe. Then stroll down the *Ramblas*, which are a series of streets joining on to each other. From the *Plaza de Cataluña* near the *Ramblas* we come to an old church, *Santa Ana* (1146, burnt down 1936). A cloister is preserved. A new church has been built beside the ruins. On the corner of *Calle del Carmen* is another church, destroyed by the Republicans, *Nuestra Señora de Belen* [2], built by the Jesuits. The following stretch of the *Rambla* is the *Estudios*, where there is a bird-market in the mornings. Then follows the *Rambla De San Jose* with its flower-market. Here also is the market hall, *Mercado de la Boqueria*, and next door the *Palacio de la Virreina*.

The *Museo de Artes Decorativas* [3] contains collections of carpets, porcelain and furniture. The building (1778) belonged to the Viceroy of Peru. *Rambla de San Jose* ends at the square, *Llano de la Boqueria*. From here the *Calle del Cardenal Casanas* leads to the *Plaza del Pino*, with the church of

Santa Maria del Pino [4] (15th-c.). Although this church has also been damaged by the war, it is worth seeing for its beautiful stained glass and a magnificent rose window. We return to *Llano de la Boqueria* and continue along the *Rambla*, now called '*Capuchinos*'. Immediately to the right is the huge theatre (5000 seats),

Gran Teatro del Liceo [5], which is the 2nd biggest opera-house and concert-hall in Europe—after the Scala in Milan. To the r. of the theatre is the *Calle de San Pablo*, leading to the Romanesque church of

San Pablo del Campo [6]. The name 'del Campo' means 'in the country' and indicates that, when it was built in 1117, it lay outside the town wall. If you have made the little detour to *San Pablo*, it is best to continue along the *Calle de San Pablo* to the *Calle del Marques del Duero*, known as '*Paralelo*', where you turn to the l. and descend to the *Plaza Puerta de la Paz* by the harbour. Otherwise continue along the *Ramblas*, cross the busy shopping centre, *Calle de Fernando* (l. of the *Ramblas*). This street leads to the square *San Jaime*, which we will mention later. The next side street to the l. is the short *Calle de Colon*, which leads to the *Plaza Real*, a lovely square with palm trees and arcades. The last stretch of the *Ramblas* is the *Rambla de Santa Monica*. It leads past the *Plaza del Teatro* to the *Plaza Puerta de la Paz*, with the

Museo Maritimo [7], the naval museum, containing numerous model ships. The building was previously a barracks. In the square is the Columbus memorial,

Monumento de Colon [8]. The tall column is crowned by a 25-ft.-high statue of the famous explorer (lift up to a platform).

We continue along the wide palm-fringed avenue, *Paseo de Colon*, to the *Plaza Antonio*

Lopez with the large general post-office. Go on along the *Paseo de Isabel II* to the *Plaza de Palacio*, a business centre. Here we find *La Lonja* [9], the stock exchange, founded in 1382. The hall is interesting. If you turn to the r. out of the *Plaza de Palacio* you will come to the fishing quarter, *Barcelonetta* (bathing beach).

From the *Plaza de Palacio* we continue

along the *Avenida del Marques de Argentera*, past the *Estacion de Francia* to the large municipal park,

Parque y Jardines de la Ciudadela [10], which is laid out on the site of the old citadel. In this lovely park is *Barcelona's Zoo*. In the SE. corner of the park is what used to be the *Palacio Real*, now used as a gallery for modern art, *Museo de Arte Moderno*, with sculptures and paintings from the 19th and 20th c.

Take a trip to the remarkable church of *Templo de la Sagrada Familia* [11]. It was begun in 1882 with money raised by charity, but it is not yet completed. The church is to have 12 towers more than 300 ft. high and a dome 525 ft. high. As yet only the crypt and the porch with 4 towers have been built.

The extraordinary modern church of La Sagrada Familia

We continue from the municipal park. Go behind the market hall, the *Merceria del Borne*, and cross the *Plaza del Borne*, which used to be the scene of festivals. All around are old, picturesque side-streets, which still retain their medieval character. We come to the church of

Santa Maria del Mar [12]. a lovely 14th-c. building with beautiful mosaic windows. After the cathedral this is the most important church in Barcelona.

Along the *Calle de Plateria* we come to the *Plaza del Angel*. We are now in the old quarter, the so-called *Barrio Chino*. Go along the *Calle de Jaime I* to the *Plaza San Jaime* [13] with the *Casa de la Diputacion* (15th c.), seat of provincial government. The adjoining building is the law courts, *Audiencia*, with a fine façade towards the *Calle del Obispo Irurita*. The town hall, *Ayuntamiento* (1369–78), is also in the Plaza San Jaime. The main façade dates from 1847, but on the l. are traces of the original style. There are two charming inner courts, the one in early Gothic and the other in late Gothic style. From one of the courts one can enter the council chamber (some fine paintings).

Go now along the *Calle del Obispo Irurita*, past the bishop's palace, *Palacio Episcopal* to the *Plaza de la Catedral* with Barcelona's cathedral,

Catedral Santa Cruz or *Santa Eulalia* [14], which was built on the highest spot of old Barcelona. The present church was built in 1298 on the site of an earlier Romanesque church. A few stone reliefs by the NE. side-porch are survivals from the original building. However the church's main front dates from 1886–98, and the dome from 1913. The interior is extraordinarily beautiful with a row of exquisite mosaic windows (15th-c. and later). In the crypt is an Italian alabaster sarcophagus, which is supposed to contain the remains of Saint Eulalia. The church treasure in the sacristy is impressive. One can ascend one of the towers (210 steps). The effort is repaid by a magnificent view. Remember to visit the adjacent cloister (palms). In the *Sala Capitular* are paintings by Spanish masters of the 14th and 15th cs.

The cathedral tower

In the cathedral square we also see the *Casa del Arcediano* (15th-c.) with its lovely 'patio'. The building houses the city archives. The *Casa Canonica* is also from the 15th c. Previously the lawcourts, it is now converted into a church museum. The *Casa Canonica* is contiguous with the former palace of the Counts of Barcelona. Here is the *Museo Mares* with Romanesque, Gothic and Renaissance sculptures. A little street *Bajada de Santa Clara* leads to the

The entrance to Montjuich Park with the buildings from the International Exhibition of 1929

Plaza del Rey [15], where the palaces of the counts of Barcelona and the kings of Aragon stood in former times. Nowadays only a 'mirador', a look-out tower, remains. Beside the *Capilla Real de Santa Agueda* is the *Casa Clariana-Padellas* with *Barcelona's city museum*.

The Plaza del Rey in the old quarter

Other things to see:

Montjuich (funicular from the Calle del Marques del Duero). This little ridge lies on the Southern outskirts of the town and presents a steep cliff face to the sea. Take a walk up there from the *Plaza de España* to the *Avenida Reina Maria Cristina*, ending in a lovely park. Keep to the r. until you come to

Pueblo Español [16], constructed for the international exhibition in 1929. This is a village of houses, characteristic of the various Spanish provinces. Each province is represented by a street in the village. A visit to *Pueblo Español* is therefore an excellent introduction to a tour of Spain. In No. 6 *Calle Pallaresa* is a museum for commercial art and crafts. Follow the outermost path, skirting *Pueblo Español*, which leads to a look-out point. Turn to the left here and return to the

Palacio Nacional [17], which contains the *Museo de Arte Cataluña*, Barcelona's most important collection of art, with works by *Zurbaran, Ribera, Velazquez* and *El Greco*. There is also an ethnographical and an *archaeological* museum [18] in the park. Walk towards the stadium and go past the Greek theatre, which lies on the l. You will also pass the station of the funicular railway, with which you can travel to the *Castillo de Montjuich* or down to '*Paralelo*' in the town. Finally you will come right out to the *Miramar* [19], from which there is a magnificent view. From here you can descend the steps to the *Plaza de Colon* by the harbour.

🚃 From *Estacion de Francia* ('*Termino*') to Valencia, Port Bou, Paris, Tarragona, Zaragoza, Madrid or Irun.

From *Estacion del Norte* ('Villanova') to Puigcerda (–Toulouse, France), Zaragoza (–Pau, France).

🚋 From the *Plaza de la Universidad* 12 to Montserrat.

From the *Calle de Diputacion* 269 to Blanes.

🏨 [A] Ritz, Avenida José Antonio 668 (L), [B] Majestic, Paseo de Gracia 70 and [C] Oriente, Rambla del Centro 20–22. 🏨 [D] Victoria, Ronda de San Pedro 2, [E] Internacional, Rambla del Centro 1, [F] Recasens, Plaza Universidad 16, and [G] Esplendido, Calle de Pelayo 8. 🏨 [H] Balmes, Calle de Balmes 7, [J] Peninsular, Calle de San Pablo 34–36, [K] Viena, Calle del Carmen 22.

▲ In the town quarter *Guinardo*: Albergue Guinardo, near the *Hospital de San Pablo*.

△ (1) Mataro (near the beach *La Bovila*). (2) San Adrian on the shore of *Besos*, Calle de Besos. (3) Between the *Palacio Nacional* and the stadium.

State Tourist office: Avenida Jose Antonio 658.

British Consulate: Jungueras 18.

TOLEDO

TOLEDO (1720 ft.; pop. 45,000) is situated on a rocky promontory in the Tagus valley with the river flowing on three sides. The narrow streets are steep and crooked, showing Moorish influence. Its history can be traced back to pre-historic times. In 192 B.C. it was conquered by the Romans, and from 712 to 1085 Toledo was in the hands of the Moors. Its inhabitants were the so-called Mozarabs, 'sham arabs': Christians, who adopted the Arabic language and some of their customs. After 1087 the town became the residence of the Castilian kings and the centre for the church. In the middle of the 16th c. Philip moved his court and government to *Madrid* and Toledo lost her prominent political position.

The town's glorious past is reflected in its many historical buildings. We shall list a few here, ordered so that they can be seen in a round tour beginning at the point where one enters the town on the road from *Madrid*.

Hospital de San Juan Bautista—the residence of the Dukes of Lerma. Begun in 1541. The chapel is interesting. Permission can be obtained to see the many treasures, including works by El Greco, Ribera, Tintoretto, Titian, etc., and an 18th-c. dispensary.

Puerta Nueva de Bisagra is the town gate of 1550.

Puerta Antigua de Bisagra, the old Bisagra-town gate, also called *Puerta de Alfonso VI*, was built by the Arabs in the 10th c.

Santiago del Arrabal, a 12th-c. church. Note the traces of Moorish influence.

Puerta del Sol is the best preserved town gate in Toledo.

Cristo de la Luz, first of all a Christian Church then an Arab mosque, is now again a church. The interior is interesting.

Santo Domingo el Real is a 14th-c. monastery church with a fine pillared façade.

Museo de San Vicente, museum for church art. Fine works by *El Greco* and his pupil, *Tristan*, also by *Ribera*. Apart from these there are tapestries from Brussels and oriental carpets, etc.

The cathedral, *Catedral de Toledo*, is the town's most interesting building. It was built (1227–1493) on the site of the former chief mosque. With the exceptions of the cathedrals in *Burgos* and *Seville* this is the most important Gothic building in Spain. There is a fine view from the N. tower. The S. tower was never completed, but instead was crowned with a Baroque cupola. The three porches in the main front were built 1418–50. Of the side-porches note in particular the richly decorated *Puerta de los Leones*. There is a daily service with the Mozarabic ritual at 10 o'clock in the *Capilla Mozarabe*. The interior is 360 ft. long and 100 ft. high. There is an altar painting by *El Greco* in the sacristy. The interesting treasure chamber is in the *Capilla de San Juan*. See also the cloisters.

Alcazar, the ruins of the former fortress, is at the highest point in the town, on the site of a Roman Castle. Early in the Civil War (1936–9) it was held in a tremendous siege by the nationalist troops—it is now a museum in memory of the war-dead.

Hospital de Santa Cruz (15th–16th c.), damaged in 1936, houses the *Museo Arqueologico* with discoveries from Roman and Visigothic excavations. An excellent collection of paintings, e.g. *Ribera* and *Murillo*.

Puenta de Alcantara is the oldest bridge over the *Tagus*, erected by the Arabs in 866 with later restorations and the addition of gate-towers.

On the other side of the river are:

The castle of San Servando (11th c. fine view).

To the tour described above may be added a visit to

San Tome, a former mosque, converted into a church in the 16th c. Here is one of El Greco's most famous works: *The Burial of Count Orgaz*.

Santa Maria la Blanca, a former synagogue (12th–13th c.), was converted into a church in 1405, used as barracks for some years at the end of the 18th c., and is now a church again. The architecture is interesting.

San Juan de los Reyes, formerly a Franciscan monastery. There is a lovely late Gothic cloister and a magnificent view from the terrace.

Sinagoga del Transito is a fine example of the Mudejar style (ca. 1365) and is extremely interesting.

Casa del Greco was the residence of the famous Cretan-born painter *Domenico Theotokopuli*, known as *El Greco*. It contains furniture and paintings, including some by *El Greco*, *Velazquez* and *Murillo*. Next door is the *Museo de Greco* with 20 original paintings and photographic reproductions of the master's other works.

A tour round Toledo along the *Carretera de Circunvalacion* is recommended.

🏨 Hotel de la Almazara, Quinta Mirabel, outside the city. Carlos V, Calle de Juan Labrador 13. 🏨 Hotel Suizo, Plaza del Zocodover 41. 🏠 Del Lino, Calle de Santa Justa 9. Maravillas, Barrio del Rey 7.

△ On the road to Aranjuez, 3 km from Toledo.

Tourist Office: Plaza de Zocodover.

Post Office: Calle de la Plata 1.

18 TOURS THROUGH SPAIN

As Spain is such a large country, there has been no attempt to cover it completely in these tours. The Editor has preferred to limit them to descriptions of those parts of the country which are of most interest to tourists. As can be seen from the map, the tours have been planned so that they connect with each other. It is therefore possible for you to plan longer or shorter journeys, according to the time at your disposal.

The tours are principally designed for those travelling by road, but railway connections are given in the itineraries and on the maps of each tour.

SUPPLEMENTARY GUIDE BOOKS

It should be possible to manage a journey through Spain solely with the help of this book, but should anyone wish for a more comprehensive guide, the following books can be recommended: Michelin's Yellow Guide *Espagne* (French); *Introducing Spain* by Cedric Salter; Nagel's *Spain and Portugal*.

SUPPLEMENTARY MAP MATERIAL

Michelin's road map, *Spain and Portugal* (2 sheets, N. & S.); Hallwag's *Iberia*; Firestone's *Cataluña* and *Costa Brava*; Foldex road map; Kummerly & Frey's *Spain-Portugal*.

INDEX TO SYMBOLS USED IN THE ITINERARIES

- 🏛 Hotel of specially good class.
- 🏛 Hotel of good standard.
- 🏛 Hotel of simple, but comfortable standard. With regard to prices see page 16.
- ▲ Youth hostel (for men only!)
- △ Camping place.
- 🚌 Rail connections. (NB: not always daily.)
- 🚍 Bus connections. (Not always daily.)
- 🛥 Ship connections.
- ✈ Air connections.

The Editor takes no responsibility for information given, regarding prices, departure times, etc., which are liable to alteration.

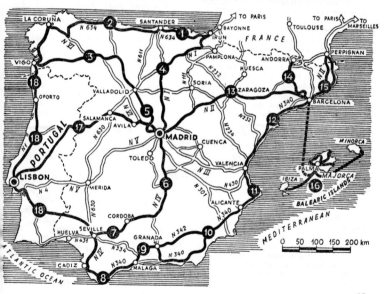

Tour 1: Irun—San Sebastian—Santander (247 km)

IRUN (pop. 18,000) lies on the Spanish frontier. The church *Nuestra Señora del Juncal* (1508, with later alterations, lovely altarpiece) and the town hall (1763) are worth seeing. Make a detour (7 km) along the *R. Bidassoa* to *Cape Higuer* (fine view from the lighthouse), passing *Fuenterrabia*, a small place with picturesque streets (view from the 12th-c. castle, *Palacio Carlos V*; festival from 7–10 Sept.).

🏨 Alcazar. 🏛 Lizaso.

In *Fuenterrabia*: 🏨 Carlos V. 🏛 Concha, and Franco.

We now drive along N1, which winds through the mountains (note *Peña de Aya*, 2652 ft., on the l.) to *Renteria* with a 16th-c. church. Visit the idyllic harbour of *Pasajes de San Juan* (3 km). Continue along the main road to

SAN SEBASTIAN (pop. 155,000), provincial capital and in summer the seat of the Spanish government and the diplomatic corps. It is beautifully situated in *La Concha Bay*, an ideal holiday centre with fine beaches. It is dominated by *Monte Urgull* (439 ft.) with *Castillo de la Mota* and by *Monte Igueldo* (598 ft.). At the foot of *Monte Urgull* is the old quarter of the town with the main street *Alameda de Calvo Sotelo*. To the W. it is bordered by the *Plaza de la Constitucion* with the town hall, housed in the former *Gran Casino*. In front of the town hall the lovely park, *Alderdi-Eder*, stretches towards the *Playa de la Concha*, one of San Sebastian's two excellent bathing-beaches.

Sights: *San Vincente church* (16th c. with

the *Gros* quarter on the other side of the *Urumea*). Then we pass (r.) the *Museo Oceanografico* or the *Palacio del Mar*, with an interesting collection of model ships and an aquarium. We are now by the harbour. From here one can sail to the island of *Santa Clara* (lighthouse).

Santa Maria (at the end of the *Calle Mayor*) is a large triple-naved church from the middle of the 17th c.

A view from Monte Igueldo towards San Sebastian with the isle of Sta Clara and Monte Urgull on the left

Excursions: (1) *Monte Urgull*. There is a path from Santa Maria, leading up the mountain. One cannot visit the fortress. (2) *Monte Igueldo*. You can take the tram to *Playa de Ondarreta* and from there take the funicular railway to the summit (598 ft.). (3) *Monte Ulia*. Take a tram through the suburb *Gros* to the foot of the hill. From here there is a lovely walk. There is a fine view from the

many alterations) is the oldest in the town. The high altar dates from 1584. Near the church on the other side of the Calle 31 de Agosto is the former monastery of *San Telmo*, which is a museum, with paintings (17th c. and modern), and a historical and ethnographical section. Now take a trip round *Monte Urgull* (fine view over *Monte Ulia* and

restaurant, *Peña del Aguila*. One can return via *Pasajes*.

State Tourist Office: in the Victoria-Eugenia theatre. *Post Office:* Calle de Garibay.

🏛 Maria Cristina, Paseo dela Republica Argentina (L) and Hispano Americano, Calle de San Martin 1. 🏛 Internacional, Calle de San Martin 39.

▲ Monte Igueldo.

△ Near the Playa de Miraconcha.

🚂 (1) On main line Irun–Madrid. (2) Bilbao–Santander.

🚌 (1) Madrid. (2) Bilbao.

We continue through a tunnel to the suburb, *Antiguo*, and along the winding road through fertile countryside until we come to some cross-roads, where we turn r. along N634. We pass *Usurbil* and follow the *R. Oria* to the fishing village of *Orio*. The road climbs in wide curves and then descends to

ZARAUZ (pop. 7000), a delightful holiday resort. Its streets are narrow with lovely old medieval buildings. From here we follow the beautiful road along the Cantabrian coast.

GUETARIA is connected by a causeway to the isle of *San Antonio* (fine view from the lighthouse).

ZUMAYA (pop. 3,500) contains a museum for painting and ceramics, housed in the former monastery of *Santiago Echea* (12th c.). At *Deva*, the main road turns inland, but we continue along the coast, despite the many bends and hills. We pass through the fishing villages of *Motrico*, *Ondarroa* and *Lequeitio* (14th–15th-c. church), and then turn l. to *Arteaga* and *Guernica*. Continue N. along the l. bank of *R. Mundaca* to

BERMEO (pop. 12,000), an important fishing-harbour. One can make a detour to *Cape Machichaco* (view). We now pass *Sollube* (2223 ft., fine view), and the road winds over the ridge of *Monte Acherre* to

BILBAO (137 km; pop. 270,000), founded at the end of the 13th c. The town lies eight miles from the mouth of the *R. Nervion*. Its harbour is extremely important and is supplemented by a docks for ocean-going ships. It is also one of the most important industrial towns in Spain. The town has little to offer tourists. Sight-seeing can be limited to the *Catedral de Santiago* (14th c.) and the *Museo de Bellas Artes*, containing some paintings by the Spanish masters.

🏛 Carlton (L.) Plaza de Federico Moyua. Tarrontequi, Arsnel 16 Alimirante, Correo 2. 🏛 Excelsior, Calle de Hurtado de Amezaga 6. 🍴 Arana, Calle Bidebarrieta 2.

State Tourist Office: Paseo del Arenal.
Post: Almeda de Urquijo 15.

🚂 (1) San Sebastian. (2) Miranda de Ebro.

🚌 (1) Santander. (2) San Sebastian.

We leave *Bilbao* along the *Gran Via Lopez de Haro* and follow road N634 to

CASTRO URDIALES (171 km; pop. 12,000). Its Gothic

church (13th–14th c.) and old castle stand on a promontory. At **SANTOÑA** (2113 km; pop. 11,000), there is a 12th–13th-c. monastery church and a fine bathing-beach.

We cross the little *R Miera*. In *Solares* the road forks r. along the coast to

SANTANDER (247
A view over Bilbao km; see tour 2).

29

Tour 2: Santander—La Coruña (540 km)

SANTANDER (pop. 130,000). With its lovely situation on a peninsula between the sea and the picturesque little bay and its mild climate, it is understandable that the town attracts many tourists. It is the capital of the province of the same name, the only coastal province of *Old Castile*.

One should see the *cathedral* (beautiful crypt of ca. 1200) and also the various museums (the prehistoric museum in the *Palacio de la Diputacion*, Calle Rubio, and the art gallery in the *Biblioteca y Museo*, Calle de la Florida). At the S. end of the harbour, *Puerto chico*, near the *Palacio de la Diputacion* is the *Estacion de Biologia Maritima*, museum and aquarium. NW. of the town is the wonderful beach *El Sardinero* with a casino, fine restaurants and hotels. Nearby is the peninsula *Magdalena* with the former royal summer residence (one may visit the park on application to the bailiff).

Excursions: (1) The *Altamira* caves (see below). (2) *Cape Mayor* and *Punteforado*, a natural bridge of limestone (3 km from Sardinero). (3) Trips into the Cantabrian mountains, e.g. to Reinosa (74 km SW.).

Hotels. *In the town:*

🏨 Bahia, Avenida de Alfonso XIII 5 (L). Rex, Avenida de Calvo Sotelo 9. 🏨 Mexico, Calle de Mendez Nunez 12. ⚓ Ignacia, Calle del General Mola 5.

On the sea-front:

🏨 Real, Paseo de Perez Galdos 20 (on hillside, 1 km from beach, L.). 🏨 Sardinero, Plaza de Italia 1. ⚓ Colon, Plaza de las Brias 1.

△ Near the lighthouse at *Sardinero*.

Tourist Office: Avenida de Alfonso XIII.

Post: Avenida de Alfonso XIII.

🚌 (1) Oviedo (2) Palencia (Burgos and Madrid).

🚊 (1) Madrid. (2) Gijon—Oviedo. (3) San Sebastian.

We leave *Santander* along N611. In the distance we can see the snow-capped peaks of the *Picos de Europa* (8586 ft.). We turn r. in *Barreda*, following the coast road to

SANTILLANA DEL MAR, with the *Parador de Gil Blas*, in a converted old mansion (interesting interior). The Romanesque *monastery church* and the monastery of *Santa Juliana* (founded in the 6th c.) are worth seeing. Nearby (2 km) are the world renowned subterranean caves of

ALTAMIRA, whose walls are decorated by life-like drawings of animals, dating from the ice-age (from 15–20,000 years old). Also visit the museum next door to the entrance, and the stalactite caves.

A prehistoric painting from the Altamira caves

Now we climb a ridge and continue along the coast road through *Comillas* (beautifully situated, with good beach) and *San Vicente* (fortress ruins, old church, large beach) to

Unquera, which is the starting-point for an excursion to the *Picos de Europa*.

We continue through the harbour town of *Llanes* (△), to *Ribadesella*, on the mouth of the *R. Sella*, and along the coast road, N634, to the large harbour town of

GIJON (pop. 135,000), pleasantly situated with a large bathing-beach, and several comfortable hotels; then round the *Cape de Peñas* and through *Aviles* (see the town hall and four old churches) to

OVIEDO (212 km; pop. 110,000), the capital of the former kingdom of Asturias, known for its *cathedral* (Gothic, begun in 1388). There is a good view from the elegant 266-ft. high tower. Visit the *Camara Santa*, containing magnificent treasure and see the cloister. Despite the damage it suffered during the Civil War, the town has preserved many other lovely buildings, e.g. the town hall: *Casa Consistorial.*

Tourist Office: Cabo Novald.

🏨 Principado, Calle de Francisco 8.

🏨 Oviedo, Calle de Covadonga 6.

▲ *Navia:* Albergue Alejandro Salazar del S.E.V.

△ In *Puerto de Pajares* (55 km towards *Leon*; 4433 ft.) at the *Parador.*

🚌 (1) Gijon. (2) Leon.

🚆 (1) Gijon. (2) Santander–Bilbao–San Sebastian. (3) La Coruña.

From *Oviedo* we drive along N634 through pleasant landscape, past *Grado* and *Salas* (an elaborate monument in the church of *Santa Maria*) to

LUARCA (303 km; pop. 25,000) with its bathing-beach. Soon afer we cross the *R. Navia.* The road is very beautiful. We go through Castropol and make a circuit round the bay, through *Vegadeo* (N640 direct to *Lugo*). The main road, N634, continues N. to *Ribadeo* and *Villalba.* Make a detour to

LUGO (31 km; pop. 55,000), capital of the province of the same name, and founded by the Romans. Take a walk round the old Roman walls, which are almost undamaged. You come to them near the *cathedral.* They were begun in A.D. 300, are over 1 mile long,

more than 30 ft. high, about 20 ft. thick, and have 85 towers and 4 gates. See also the *cathedral.*

Tourist Office: Plaza de España 27.

🏨 Mendez Nunez, Calle de la Reina 1.

▲ Santa Domingo 9.

From *Lugo* we rejoin the road from *Villalba* towards *La Coruña* at *Baamonde*, continue along N.VI through *Betanzos* and over the *R. Mendo.* The road climbs a little and then descends with a wonderful view over the harbour to

LA CORUÑA (540 km; pop. 150,000), capital of the province, and situated in the north-western- most corner of Spain. It is an important port, picturesquely situated on a rocky peninsula. It was a prehistoric settle- ment, and it was from here that part of the 'Invincible Ar- mada' sailed against England in 1588.

The Tower of Her- cules at La Coruña, founded by the Romans

In the old quarter is the town hall (*Ayuntamiento*) with a collection of mod- ern paintings, and the churches of *Santiago* (Romanesque with Gothic additions) and *Santa Maria del Campo*, both dating from ca. 13th c.

Tourist Office: Darsena de la Olarina.

🏨 Finisterre (L.), Paseo del Parrote, Marineda, Calle de Rosalia de Castro 13.

🏨 Atlantico, Paseo de Mendez Nunez.

🏨 Primitiva Luz, Calle de Franja 40.

🚌 Lugo–Leon.

🚆 (1) Santiago. (2) Ribadeo–Oviedo

Tour 3: La Coruña—Santiago—Leon—Valladolid (674 km)

The most attractive way to *Santiago* is via *Cape Finisterre* (about 200 km, bad road). By the direct route, N550, it is only 65 km. The road passes through the *Galician Mountains* (gradients up to 1 in 10).

SANTIAGO DE COMPOSTELA (65 km; pop. 62,000), previously the capital of the kingdom of *Galicia*, has, since the 11th century, been the most frequented place of pilgrimage in Spain. Its most interesting building is the famous

Cathedral (1060–1211), built on the site of the earlier basilica, which was erected in memory of *St James* the Apostle whose remains were discovered in the old town of *Iria Flavia* in the 9th c. The church is the finest Romanesque building in Spain. The west front, the *Obradoiro*, is a magnificent baroque façade, flanked by two tall towers (250 ft.). On the gable between them is St James's statue. The S. porch, the *Puerta de Plateiras*, besides the *Torre de la Trinidad* (245 ft. view), is also extraordinarily beautiful. Here we enter the church. The richly ornamented *high altar* stands above the apostle's *silver coffin*, which may be seen. Behind the *Obradoiro* is the *Portico de la Gloria*, a three-bayed porch with elaborate decoration.

Beside the S. porch is the entrance to the lovely cloister. The large staircase is built

The *Plaza de España* is moreover surrounded by beautiful old buildings. Opposite the cathedral stands the town hall, the *Palacio Consistorial* (1766–67), and on the N. side of the square is the *Hospital Real* (1489), now a luxury hotel known as the *Hostal de los Reyes Catolicos* (). North of the cathedral is the former monastery of *San Martin Pinario* with four interesting cloisters.

A view of the Cathedral of Santiago de Compostela

Other interesting churches in Santiago are *Santo Domingo* (tower with exterior staircase) and *Santa Maria la Real del Sar* (situated in the southern suburb, *Horreo*) a Romanesque building of 1147.

Tourist Office: Rua del Villar 43.

We continue along the main road N550, through *Padron* (the Roman *Iria Flavia*, see above) and *Caldas de Reyes*, whose sulphur springs were known even in Roman times.

over the *Catedral Vieja*, the old cathedral (12th c.). Adjoining the cathedral is the *Palacio Arzobispal*, the archbishop's palace.

PONTEVEDRA (122 km; pop. 35,000), capital of the province, is beautifully situated beside the rivers *Lerez* and *Tomeza* where they flow into the *R. Pontevedra*. See the three lovely churches: the monastery of *San Francisco*, and the chapel of *La Peregrina* (a round church, erected in 1776), both on the *Plaza Mayor* and—much the most striking

La Peregrina at Pontevedra

—the Gothic church of *Santa Maria la Mayor* (1550), in the old quarter, to the E. The ruins of the monastery of *Santo Domingo* (museum) are also worth seeing.

Tourist Office: Michelena 27.

🏨 Parador del Baron. ⌂ Engracia.

S. through lovely scenery with vineyards, we soon come in sight of *Vigo Bay*, on the S. shore of which lies

VIGO (157 km; pop. 160,000), famous for its sardine fishing fleet, beautifully situated, surrounded by ridges (two of these crowned with fortresses) and only 40 km from the Portuguese frontier. The old quarter, leading off from the *San Francisco* beach, is in peculiar contrast to the skyscrapers of the newer part of the town. Go down to the fishermen's quarter of *Berbes*, and see the bustle of the market. There is a good view from the *Castillo del Castro* (400 ft.). The tour by boat to the islands in *Vigo Bay* is recommended.

Tourist Office: Pardines de Elduayen.

🏨 Moderno, Policargo Sanz. 1.

🚢 (1) Santiago. (2) Orense–Leon. (3) Oporto.

We continue along N120, through the mountain scenery of the *Sierra del Suido* (rising to 2500 ft.). After *Ribadavia* the road follows the pretty *Minho* valley to

ORENSE (263 km; pop. 50,000), the provincial capital. Near the *Plaza Mayor* in the centre of the old quarter is the cathedral of *San Martin*, the main part of which dates from 1218–48. The interior is very beautiful. The 12th-c. bishop's palace on the *Plaza Mayor*, a *Museo Provincial*, contains a valuable archaeological collection. See also the Romanesque church, *La Trinidad* (13th c.), with its two towers. The huge bridge over the *Minho* (the span of the middle arch is 140 ft.,

height 125 ft.) was originally built in 1230 and the middle section was renewed in 1667.

🏛 del Parque, Parque de San Lazaro 23.

We continue along N120, which ascends the *Alto de Rodicio* (3100 ft.) to *Puebla de Trives*. In wide curves it continues downwards, following an old Roman road (Roman bridge in *Petin*). We now pass through *Barco de Valdeorras* (coal-mines) beside the *R. Sil*. We leave *Galicia* and drive into *Leon*. In *Ponferrada* road N VI (from La Coruña) joins N120, which we follow to

ASTORGA (494 km; pop. 15,000). The *town hall* is 17th-c., the *cathedral* 15th–16th c., with towers from the 18th c.

We continue by N120 to

LEON (541 km; 2671 ft.; pop. 65,000). The town originated as a Roman camp in A.D. 100 and it took the name of the Roman legion. *Leon* is known for its many beautiful buildings and above all for its cathedral, *Santa Maria de Regla* (13th–14th c.), one of the best examples of High Gothic in Spain. The west front is most interesting. There is a central gable with a large rose window, flanked by two towers (210 and 220 ft.). The church's interior is also made beautiful by the finest stained-glass windows in Spain. From the cathedral

Leon Cathedral

follow the old Roman city wall (many towers) to *Puerta del Castillo* continuing across the *Plaza del Castillo* to the church of *San Isadoro* (10th–11th c.), one of the chief examples of Romanesque in Spain. See also the *Capilla Mayor* and the treasure house. In the suburb *Renueva* is the beautiful monastery (1530–1719) of *San Marcos*.

Tourist Office: Plaza de la Catedral 4.

🏨 Oliden, Plaza de Santo Domingo 5.

🏨 Regina, Avenida de la Independencia 6.

⌂ Paris, Calle del Generalisimo Franco 20.

▲ Villafranca 5.

🚢 (1) Orense. (2) Oviedo. (3) Valladolid. (4) La Coruña.

🚂 (1) Madrid. (2) Burgos.

We now follow N601 through *Medina de Rioseco*, with the church of *Santa Maria de Mediavilla* with Capilla de Benavente (1546), to **VALLADOLID** (674 km; see tour 5).

Tour 4: Irun—Burgos—Aranda de Duero—Madrid (491 km)

From **IRUN** (see tour 1) to *Burgos* one can either drive via *Bilbao–Santander* (see tour 1) or, as here, take the shorter way via *Vitoria* and *Miranda de Ebro*. In either case we come first to **SAN SEBASTIAN** (see tour 1). About 8 km further on the road forks and we take N1 past the *Parador Bidarte* (🏨), and after a few small towns reach

TOLOSA (44 km; pop. 15,000) on the *R. Oria*, which we follow. On the l. is the mountain, *Aralar* (4538 ft.). After *Villafranca* keep to the l. at the fork and drive through pleasant countryside towards the pass of

PUERTO DE ECHEGARATE (2080 ft.). There is a fine view over the *Navarra* plateau and towards the mountain ranges of *Sierra de San Adrian* and *Sierra de Aralar*. In *Alsasua* we turn r. On the r. you see the peak of *Monte Araz* (4894 ft.) and behind that, *Monte Aitzgorri* (5042 ft.). Just before *Salvatierra* there is a footpath, leading to some prehistoric burial places (at *Eguilaz*). We now follow the road over the *Alava plateau*, a very fertile territory. We still have mountains in the background. We pass the ruins of a fortress, and just before *Vitoria* see the Romanesque basilica-church *Estibaliz* (12th c.) on a ridge.

The Cathedral of Burgos

VITORIA (133 km; 1900 ft.; pop. 60,000), the capital of the province of *Alava*, is a well-known holiday resort with narrow streets and many lovely old houses. See the *Catedral Santa Maria* (14th c.) with a beautiful pillared entrance-hall and a 17th-c. tower. There are other interesting churches in the town.

🏨🏨 Fronton, Calle de San Prudencio 7.
🏨 Francia, Calle de Dato 39.

🚂 On main line Irun–Madrid.

The road continues through beautiful countryside, passing through the old fortified town of *La Puebla de Arganzon*, whose circular wall is still intact.

MIRANDA DE EBRO (167 km; 1508 ft.) is an important traffic centre. The church of *San Nicolas* (12th c.) is a former mosque with an attractive Moorish porch. On the r. bank of the *R. Ebro* are the ruins of an old fortress, *Casa Consistorial* (1778). The road goes over the *Obarenes* mountains and we come through the narrow, exciting *Pancorbo* pass near the town of the same name (picturesque fortress ruins).

BRIVIESCA (204 km; 2356 ft.) has retained its original fortifications, and the streets still have a medieval appearance. See the 16th-c. church of *Santa Clara* with its lovely carved altar-piece.

The road climbs over the pass of *Puerta la Brujula* (3188 ft.; △) to

BURGOS (246 km; 2779 ft.; pop. 85,000), provincial capital and one of Spain's most famous cities. In the 10th and 11th cs. it was the capital of the kingdom of *Old Castile* and during the Civil War the headquarters of the nationalists. Its beautiful cathedral, *Catedral de Santa Maria*, was begun in 1221 and after only 9 years the huge church was consecrated. The open-work spires, however, were not added until 1442–58 (built by *Johann of Cologne*). The main front faces the *Plaza de Santa Maria;* over the large rose window are the statues of 8 kings. The other porches are also beautifully decorated. The interior with its magnificent *octagonal cupola* and many side-chapels is overwhelming; see also the lovely cloister. In the *Plaza de Santa Maria* is the church of *San Nicolas* (also built by *Johann of Cologne* in 1408, restored in 1911). On the other side of the cathedral is the *Plaza del Rey Fernando.* Here stands the *Santa Maria Arch*, a huge gate, flanked by two semicircular towers. The building houses part of Burgos Province's archaelogical museum. We go through the arch and across the bridge, *Puente de Santa Maria.* Turn to the l. beside the river and afterwards to the r. along the *Calle de Celera.* Here are two fine mansions: No. 27 *Casa de Angulo* and No. 29 *Casa de Miranda*.

Return to the river and follow it, turning to the l. over the next bridge, pass the theatre and the provincial government building (*Diputacion*) until you come to the *Plaza Mayor* with the town hall (*Ayuntamiento*) (1788–91). Some interesting rooms.

Other sights: the churches of *San Gil* (14th c.) and of *San Esteban* (1280 and later) and the ruins of the *Castillo*, where there

The Santa Maria Gate in Burgos

is a fine view from the bastion. Walking from San Esteban to the fortress you pass the *Arco de San Esteban* and on the way down from the ruins you pass the *Arco de San Martin*, a gate from the old

Santa Maria at Aranda de Duero

wall and *Solar del Cid*, the old churchyard.

Excursions: (1) *Monasterio de las Huelgas*,

originally a summer residence of the Castilian kings, later a convent, with an attractive church of 1249. (2) Nearby is the *Hospital del Rey*, an interesting old pilgrim's hostel (beautiful porches in Plateresque style). (3) *Cartuja de Miraflores*, a large monastery (1441). Ladies are admitted to the church only, which is very beautiful.

Tourist Office: Paseo del Espolon.

🏨 Condestable, Calle de Vitoria 7, and El Cid, Gamonal del Rio Pico. 🏨 España, Espolon 32. 🏨 Norte y Londres, Plaza de Alonso Martinez 1.

🚂 (1) on main line Irun–Madrid. (2) Palencia. (3) Zaragoza. 🚌 Santander.

We drive on along N1, past the side-road leading to the Benedictine monastery of *Santo Domingo de los Silos* (ca. A.D. 593; men can spend the night here), and through **LERMA**, surrounded by an old town wall, with large castle (17th c.) and a 17th-c. monastery church, to

ARANDA DE DUERO (328 km; pop. 10,000). The lovely church of *Santa Maria la Real* was started by the architect, *Simon of Cologne.*

🏨 Hosteria Castilla. 🏨 *Albergue* de Carretera.

At *Boceguillas* you could leave the main road and continue via *Segovia.*

Road N1 goes on through beautiful scenery of the *Sierra de Guadarrama* to the *Puerto de Somosierra* (5770 ft.). *Buitrago del Lozoya* is an old, fortified town with its medieval town walls intact. In *Lozoyuela* you should turn off from the main road and take the 10 km longer way through *Torrelaguna* and *El Molar* to

MADRID (491 km; see p. 17).

Tour 5: Valladolid—Segovia—El Escorial—Madrid (217 km)

VALLADOLID (pop. 155,000) is the capital of the province and an important traffic centre. It was here that King Ferdinand ('the Catholic') married Queen Isabella in 1469 and Christopher Columbus spent his last years (d. 1506).

The huge *cathedral* was begun in 1580, but was never completed; of the four projected corner towers only one was finished. It collapsed in 1841, but was re-erected 1880–5. The interior of the church is 400 ft. long. The *high altar* is decorated by Velazquez's picture, *The Ascension*. In the *sacristy* there is a magnificent silver-plated tabernacle, 6 ft. high (1590), whose main theme is 'Adam and Eve in Paradise'. See also the *University*, with a Baroque façade (1715), and behind it the *Colegio de Santa Cruz*: library and archaeological collection. There is also an excellent collection of wood-carvings of the 16th and 17th cs. But above all you should visit the *Colegio de San Gregorio* (1488–96) with its magnificent Gothic front and cloister, and the *Museo Nacional de Escultura Religiosa*: a marvellous collection of painting and polychromatic sculpture. Near the museum is the lovely church of *San Pablo* (1486–92) with a fine porch. Opposite the church is the 16th-c. *Palacio Real*, a former royal palace.

The cloister of San Gregorio

Tourist Office: Angustias 1.

🏨 Conde Ansurez (L.), Calle de Dona Maria de Molina 9. 🏨 Florido, Maria de Molina 7. 🏨 Inglaterra, Calle de Dona Maria de Molina 2.

🚆 (1) on main line Irun–Madrid. (2) Salamanca. (3) Leon–La Coruña. (4) Zaragoza.

🚌 (1) Madrid. (2) Leon.

We take N601 over the canal and the *R. Duero* to

CUELLAR (a partially well-preserved town wall and many lovely buildings). We cross the *R. Cega* and, driving through pleasant scenery, reach

SEGOVIA (110 km; 3250 ft.; pop. 38,000).

The town is known for its huge Roman *aqueduct*, built in the time of the Emperor Trajan. It was used to bring water from the *Fuenfria* mountains to *Segovia* (17 km). 119 immense arches, up to 150 ft. high, still stand. They are constructed of granite without the use of mortar. One part of the aqueduct has two tiers. You can climb up to it from the *Plaza de Azoguejo*, the town's traffic centre. The inner town is still surrounded by a wall, which in the NW. leads to the old fortress of the *Alcazar* (11th-c.). In the centre of the old quarter is the

Segovia, with the Cathedral in the centre and the Alcazar on the right

Cathedral, built 1525–93 in late Gothic style. The impressive 300 ft.-high *belfry* was completed in 1558. The beautiful interior is divided into three naves and measures 350 ft. long, 125 ft. wide and 100 ft. high. The lovely *cloister* is partially built of material from the old cathedral, which stood near the *Alcazar*. You may visit the church museum: works in gold, tapestries and paintings, etc.

Other interesting churches are *San Esteban*, *San Millan* (12th c., Romanesque) and *San Clemente*. Not far from *San Esteban* is *El Arco de Santiago*, an old town gate. Passing through it, we come to the *R. Eresma*. To the l. on the river bank is the *Casa de la Moneda*, the old mint, where all Spanish money was coined up to 1730. On the r. bank is the large monastery *El Parral*. To the N. is the old octagonal church of *Vera Cruz*, erected by the Knights Templar in 1208, the town hall (*Ayuntamiento*), and the church of *San Miguel* (Gothic, lovely Flemish triptych).

Excursions: *La Granja*, a Royal Palace with a lovely park, and a good collection of paintings (see below).

Tourist Office: Plaza General Franco 8.

🏨 Las Sirenas, Calle de Juan Bravo 30.

🏛 Comercio Europeo, Calle de Meliton Martin 3. ⬢ Victoria, Plaza del Generalisimo Franco 5.

△ By the *Peñalara* lake, near *La Granja*.

▲ Coca, Luis Moscardo, *Castillo*.

🚌 (1) Madrid. (2) Medina del Campo–Valladolid or Salamanca.

🚃 (1) Madrid. (2) Segovia.

We drive towards the *Guardarrama* mountains along road N601 to

LA GRANJA (122 km; 3757 ft.). The town is pleasantly situated, and is known for its palace, a royal residence, with a large park laid out with numerous artistic fountains. It is sometimes called the Spanish

Versailles, being built by Louis XIV's grandson. The road continues through forest beside the *R. Valsain* (very rocky, △) and ascends to the pass of

PUERTO DE NAVACERRADA (6000 ft.), a busy winter-sports centre, surrounded by high mountains. Soon after the road forks (N601 continues to *Madrid*). We keep to the r. and make a detour (17 km longer) crossing N VI to

EL ESCORIAL (168 km), known on account of its huge palace-monastery (1563–95). The palace is 676 ft. long and 527 ft. wide. The central part is made up of a church, whose dome and two towers rise above the high wall. The building's official name is *El Monasterio de San Lorenzo del Escorial*. The builder was given the task of creating a work which would serve four purposes: those of monastery, church, pantheon, and royal summer residence.

El Escorial

There is free entrance to the church between 7 a.m. and 6 p.m. There is an entrance fee to visit the palace and mausoleum between 10 a.m. and 6 p.m. That a visit will take some time will be realized from these figures: there are 16 towers, 1110 outer windows, 86 staircases and 2800 doors! You should visit the *sacristy* of the church and the *chapter house* of the monastery. Afterwards you can climb to the *Silla de Felipe Segundo*, a seat cut in the stone of some rocks from which the king used to see how the construction of the *Escorial* was proceeding. In front of the *Escorial* are the *Jardines del Principe* with the *Casita del Principe* (1772, museum for old furniture, porcelain and paintings).

Now it is only 49 km to

MADRID (see p. 18).

Tour 6: Madrid—Aranjuez—Valdepeñas—Cordoba (402 km)

Now we go to *Andalusia*! We leave *Madrid* along N IV, and soon see ahead of us (l.) the conical-shaped hill,
CERRO DE LOS ANGELES (2177 ft.). It lies at the geographical centre of the Peninsula, and so is called 'El Punto' (The Navel). On the summit is a 30-ft. high statue of Christ (beautiful view). Make a little detour to it (1 km).

ARANJUEZ (47 km; pop. 25,000). On the same road we soon come to the 18th-c. *Royal Palace*, with its lovely *gardens*. Near them is the *Casa del Labrador*, a little palace (1803), furnished and decorated in the Louis XVI style. There are some lovely ceiling paintings. The 'Casa' is set in the heart of a great forest of 100-ft. tall plane trees.

The Royal Palace at Aranjuez

At *Ocaña* (a small town, showing Moorish influence) the road forks (see map). We keep to N IV. Notice on a ridge the peculiar church of the town of *La Guardia*. In this town you will see many cave dwellings.

Now we drive into the landscape of *Don Quixote*, *La Mancha*, the large plain which stretches as far as the mountains of the *Sierra Morena*. Just before *Madridejos* you will see examples of the characteristic windmills, described by Cervantes in *Don Quixote*.

Just beyond *Manzanares*, with its magnificent castle, we pass an *Albergue* (🏠).

VALDEPEÑAS (200 km; pop. 26,000) is famous for its white wine. We continue over the pass of *Puerto de Despeñaperros* (fine

A typical windmill of La Mancha

view), which forms the frontier between *Castile* and *Andalusia*.

In *Santa Helena* (2411 ft.) there is a good hotel and restaurant. *Bailen* is an important road centre (*Alberque* 🏠). We come to the *Guadalquivir* valley after driving through extensive olive groves. If you have time, take a trip to the shrine of *Virgen de la Cabeza* (*Parador* 🏠). *Andujar*, on N IV, is known for its production of clay pitchers, used for wine and water. We cross the *R. Guadalquivir* and drive ca. 80 km along the l. bank to

CORDOBA (403 km; pop. 190,000), the fourth largest town in *Andalusia* and an episcopal residence. It was founded by the Romans and taken in A.D. 1711 by the Arabs, whose influence can still be seen today. Its great period was when the Calif made it his capital, especially under Abd-er-Rahman III (912–61).

Walking through the narrow streets you will enjoy peeping into the lovely flower-filled 'patios' —but it is primarily the huge

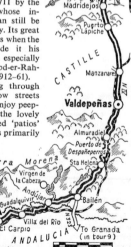

Mosque (now the cathedral), which attracts tourists' attention. It is 580 ft. long and 440 ft. wide. The oldest part dates from the 8th c. and it was extended in the 11th c. It was one of the world's greatest mosques, only the great mosque of Mecca being larger. In the 16th c. a cathedral was built into the mosque, which to some extent spoilt the original purity of style. The block, of which the *Patio de los Naranjos* with orange trees and palms forms about a third of the area, is surrounded by a high wall. 850 marble pillars with vaults of white stone and red brick support the ceiling. The 200-ft.-high belfry (view) dates from 1593. The interior is 35 ft. high and with the many pillars it gives the effect of a labyrinth.

The interior of the great Mosque of Cordoba

The fortress of Manzanares

Opposite the NW. side of the Mosque is the *Bishop's palace* and the priest's seminary, *San Pelagio*. Behind it, in the picturesque quarter of *Barrio de la Juderia* (the Ghetto), is the square, *Camposanto de los Martires*, where it is supposed that Christians were martyred. Here also we see the huge walls and towers of the *Alcazar* (now a prison). The Guadalquivir is crossed by the *Roman Bridge*, which has 16 arches. The foundations originate from Roman times, but the bridge itself is Moorish.

Cordoba's art gallery, *Museo Provincial de Bellas Artes*, and the *Museo de Julio Romero de Torres*, with its good collection of paintings (Goya, Murillo, Ribera and others, including the Cordoba-born *Antonio del Castillo y Saavedra*), are worth a visit.

The commercial centre is mainly around the *Paseo del Gran Capitan* with its leading hotels and restaurants, and the *Plaza de Jose Antonio*.

🏨 Cordoba Palace (L.); Jardines de la Victoria. Simon, Paseo del Gran Capitan 5.

🏨 Avenida and Regina, Av. del Generalismo 26 and 25. 🏨 Andalucia, Calle de Jose Zorrilla 3.

▲ Calle Alfonso VIII 18, and Calle Adarve 2.

Tourist Office: Av. del Gran Capitan 13.

🚆 (1) on main line Madrid–Seville. (2) Malaga. 🚌 (1) Seville. (2) Granada.

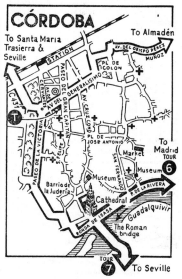

Tour 7: Cordoba—Seville (138 km)

We leave *Cordoba* by the Roman Bridge and follow N IV. *Ecija* was founded by the Romans (interesting church and plaza). *Carmona* is dominated by an old fortress. The tour passes through a fertile landscape, with large olive groves and vineyards, owned by wealthy landlords—the feudal system still partially exists here—and we soon reach the lovely capital of *Andalusia*,

SEVILLE (138 km; pop. 410,000), Spain's fourth largest town. It is connected with the sea by canals, joining the *Guadalquivir*. The canals can be navigated even by ocean-going ships. It is therefore a port, although 87 km from the sea.

A prehistoric settlement, it later became Roman and then Moorish. The Saint King Ferdinand III (of Castile) liberated the town in 1248 and made it his residence. Later came Peter I (the Cruel), and there are many strange tales of his rule. Columbus entered Seville after his first voyage to America.

You will be greatly attracted by the markedly Andalusian character of the town. On account of the warm climate the inhabitants spend much of the nights in the open: in the lovely *patios*, generally ornamented by fountains. The most typical quarter is *Santa Cruz*, stretching beside the walls of the *Alcazar*, near the famous cathedral tower, the *Giralda*. There are narrow streets of neat

The lovely cathedral tower, La Giralda, at Seville

white houses with flowers in their ornamental metal window-grilles. It is like a fairy-tale town, especially if one takes a horse cab through *Santa Cruz* in the evening.

Twice a year, Seville is turned upside down: in Easter week and during the *Feria* in April. Visitors come from all over Spain and abroad. Hotels are allowed to double their prices, but the Feria is an experience which you will long remember. In Easter Week there are colourful religious processions, and in the Feria there is dancing and music day and night.

Sights. The numbers in square brackets refer to the plan.

The *town hall* [1] is in the former bullfighting square, the *Plaza de Falange Española*. It is a Renaissance building (1527–64), a good example of the Plateresque style.

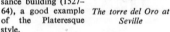

The torre del Oro at Seville

The *cathedral* [2] (1402–1506) on the site of the former chief mosque. The porches are beautiful. The tower, *La Giralda*, has become a landmark (300 ft.). It was erected (1184–96) as a minaret and was provided with a belfry in 1568. The view is impressive, especially in the evening (it is too hot in the day-time). Don't forget to go into the immense church:

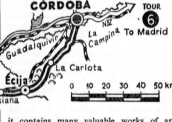

it contains many valuable works of art. From the church you can continue into the *Patio de los Naranjos*.

The *Alcazar* [3], built 1350–69, under Peter I (the Cruel), with later extensions. After the earthquake of 1755 and the fire of 1762, which caused much damage, the *Alcazar* was later re-built. One may visit it (guide). There are some pleasant rooms and patios as well as gardens (subterranean baths).

La Lonja [4], the stock exchange (1583–98), is a Renaissance building, containing the *Archivo General de las Indias:* 40,000 volumes of manuscripts and books, giving the administrative details of the New World from the time America was discovered.

Barrio de Santa Cruz [5], the former Ghetto, is now an aristocratic residential quarter, characterized by its formal beauty.

Casa de Pilatos [6] (16th c.), the house of the pilots who brought the ships up the river from the sea. It has a fine patio.

The *Church of St Gil* [7], in the N. quarter, contains the famous image known as the Virgin de la Macarena which is carried in the Holy Week processions. (Apply to keeper of souvenir stall to left of entrance.)

Museo de Bellas Artes is a section of the *Museo Provincial* [8], containing a precious collection of paintings.

Torre del Oro [9], a tower for storing the Royal Treasure, the lower part from 1220.

Parque de Maria Luisa [10], a lovely 18th-c. park with some interesting buildings from the Spanish-American exhibition (1929–30).

Triana [11], the gipsy quarter. Here are many ceramic works, which may be visited.

Tourist Office: Av. Quiepo de Llano 13.

🏛 [A] Alfonso XIII (L.), San Fernando 2. [B] Maria Cristina (L.), Jardines Cristina (roof-terrace and cellar with Andalusian flamenco dancers). [C] Colon, Canalejas 1. [D] Hotel Inglaterra, Plaza Nueva 11. 🏛 [E] Royal, Plaza Nueva 19. 🏛 [F] Cecil-Oriente, Plaza Nueva 8. [G] Marquez, Plaza Nueva 15.

🚂 *Estacion de Cordoba* (Plaza de Armas): (1) Cordoba–Madrid. (2) Huelva. (3) Merida. *Estacion de Cadiz* (San Bernardo): (1) Jerez–Cadiz. (2) Malaga. (3) Granada. (4) Algeciras.

🚌 (1) Algeciras. (2) Cadiz. (3) Cordoba. (4) Granada. (5) Huelva–Ayamonte. (6) Jerez. (7) Malaga. (8) Merida. (9) Ronda. (10) Rosal. (11) Valencia.

Tour 8: Seville—Jerez—Cadiz—Malaga (424 km)

We leave *Seville* along the l. bank of the *Guadalquivir* beside the *Parque Maria Luisa*. Later N IV crosses the tributary *Guadaira*. We are now in the Andalusian lowlands: fertile land with cornfields and olive groves, alternating with orange orchards and cotton fields, divided by cactus hedges, and many farms, devoted to breeding fighting bulls.

JEREZ DE LA FRONTERA (97 km; pop. 122,000) is a charming town, characterized by its palm avenues, is known primarily as the home of *Sherry*. Here you will find one '*Bodega*' after another. Many of the shippers allow tourists to look round (interesting). Two of the best known Sherry firms are *Gonzalez Byass* and *Pedro Domecq*. Refuse any offers from 'guides'; apply directly to the business offices.

The Colegiata Church at Jerez

From *Puerto de Santa Maria* we can look right across the bay to the lovely white town of *Cadiz*. Notice the church, *Iglesia Mayor Principal* (13th and 17th c.) and the ruins of the Moorish fortress, *San Marcos*. (Bathing— △.)

We cross the *R. Guadalete* and later the *R. de San Pedro*. On the beach you will see pyramid-shaped heaps of salt between small dyked areas. Sea water is let into these and left to dry in the sun so as to extract the salt.

Puerto Real is another very old town. From here you can really enjoy the view of Cadiz, set on a tongue of land. We come to a cross-roads, the l. fork leading to *Algeciras*, and continue straight ahead to

CADIZ (151 km; pop. 115,000), surrounded by a 50-ft-high wall, as a protection against the sea (strong tide). The typical white

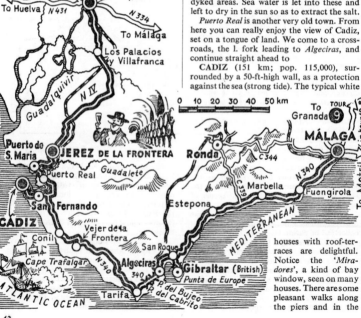

houses with roof-terraces are delightful. Notice the '*Miradores*', a kind of bay window, seen on many houses. There are some pleasant walks along the piers and in the lovely gardens with their many palms. In the *Capilla Santa Catalina* is one of Murillo's most famous works, *The Betrothal of St Catharine* and other paintings. See also the *old* and *new cathedrals*, and the *Academia de Bellas Artes*, which besides paintings has an interesting archaeological section.

Tourist Office: Calderon de la Barca 1.

🏨 Atlantico, Parque Genoves. 🏨 Francia y Paris, Plaza Calvo Sotelo 2. Plaza, right on the great bathing-beach of La Victoria. ⚓ San Francisco, Calle de Valenbuela 1.

△ (1) *Puerta de Santa Maria*. (2) *Chiclana de la Frontera*, on the road to Algeciras.

🚌 (1) Jerez-Seville. (2) Algeciras.

A view over Cadiz with the Cathedral and harbour

We now return to the cross-roads just after *San Fernando*, turn r. along N340 and soon pass *Chiclana de la Frontera* (△), where a side-road leads to the small town of *Conil*. Notice *Cape Trafalgar*, which gave its name to Nelson's famous victory. At a distance we pass the hill-top fortress town of *Vejer de la Frontera* (△). Make a detour to see it.

We drive by forests of cork-oak and pine, and olive-groves. The district is surrounded by mountains and we can soon see across the Straits of Gibraltar to the mountains of *Morocco*. We come right down to the sea—with a wonderful view. Here is the little Moorish-looking town of *Tarifa*, the Southernmost town in Europe, situated on a little peninsula, the *Punta Marroqui*. From here it is only 14 km to *Cape Cires* in *Africa*.

The road climbs past the inn, *Hosteria Tarifa*, in wide curves to *Puerto del Cabrito* (fine view over Gibraltar to the African coast). We descend past a camping place and then climb once more over a pass, *Puerto del Bujeo*, (view) and finally down to

ALGECIRAS (265 km; pop. 56,000), an important port for connections with **Tangier**, the United States, and Africa, and for cork export. Good bathing beach. Moorish ruins.

Tourist Office: On the Quay.

🏨 Reina Cristina [L.], S. of the town. 🏨 Solimar (bungalow-hotel), 4½ km N. of the town. 🏨 Marina Victoria, Avenida Canonero Danto 7.

△ On the S. beach.

🚌 (1) Cadiz. (2) Seville. (3) Malaga.

If you are going straight on you should first drive down to the harbour, after which you rejoin N340, and later pass the little town of *San Roque*. The main road continues to *Malaga* but we suggest a detour to

GIBRALTAR. The British naval and military base is on a rocky peninsula, connected to the mainland by an isthmus. The town is on the W. side of the rock, where the cliffs slope down to the sea, whereas on the other side they are perpendicular. There are Barbary apes on the rock of Gibraltar, the only place in Europe where they are wild.

🏨 Rock Hotel (L.), Europa Road 3. Bristol. 🏨 Victoria, Main Street 32, and Continental, Turnbull's Lane 3.

We return to N340. The road continues along the coast through varied landscape. We pass the small fishing town of *Estepona* and then the bungalow-hotel, Santa Marta (🏨). A little further on is the side-road C339 to

RONDA (52 km), an idyllically situated mountain town with Spain's oldest bullfighting arena. Hotel Victoria (🏨).

We again pass a bungalow-hotel, El Rodeo (🏨), and a little further on the attractive Marbella-Club (🏨).

Part of a street in Ronda

MARBELLA is a popular seaside resort. Alhamar (🏨 (L.)), good food, wonderful garden down to the beach.

TORREMOLINOS is another very popular resort, only 14 km from *Malaga*, with a magnificent, sandy beach. 🏨 Hotel Lloyd; 🏨 Hotel Montemar; ⚓ Auto Hotel. △ But there are many other good hotels all along the coast from *Marbella* to **MALAGA** (424 km; see tour 9).

Tour 9: Malaga—Granada (134 km)

MALAGA (pop. 290,000) is a wonderful holiday resort, situated in a fertile plain, the *Hoya de Malaga*, where oranges, cotton, sugar-cane, bananas, figs and vines are cultivated. The grapes are used partly for raisins, an important export commodity, and partly for wine, especially the sweet wine, which is known and valued the world over. The climate is very mild, and Malaga is ideal for holidaying or convalescing, even in winter.

Places of Interest:

The cathedral was begun in 1538, to replace the former mosque; it was damaged during the earthquake of 1680. In 1719 the work of reconstruction was begun, but was never completed. Fine view from the N. tower (250 ft.). The interior is interesting, especially the statues of saints on the finely ornamented choir-stalls.

The *Alcazaba* is a ruined Moorish fortress, built on the site of the earliest settlement (magnificent view). See the *Torre de la Vela*, the *Arco de Cristo*, the flower-filled patios, the gardens with small pools and the archaeological museum. From here climb up to *Gibralfaro* (cliff with a lighthouse), ruins of a 14th-c. fortress with a fine gate and an old mosque (restaurant, terrace, fine view).

Excursion: *Hacienda de San Jose* and *La Concepcion* (14 km), beautiful gardens with tropical plants and the remains of a Roman garden.

Tourist Office: Larios S.

🏛 Miramar (L.), Paseo de Reding 8. Belair (just outside the town), Monte de Sancha. 🏛 Limonar, Paseo del Limonar 2. 🏛 Cataluña, Paseo del Obispo 2.

🚌 (1) Ronda–Algeciras. (2) Cordoba–Seville. (3) Granada–Almeria.

🚐 (1) Algeciras. (2) Granada. (3) Seville. (4) Ronda.

We leave by N321 over the *Montes de Malaga* (view), through two tunnels and over the pass of *Puerto de Leon* (3250 ft.). From *Colemar* one can make a detour to *Villanueva*

de la Concepcion. In *Loja* are ruins of a Moorish fortress. From here there is direct road with magnificent views to *Seville* (257 km). The mountains of the Sierra Nevada soon appear and we see

GRANADA (134 km; pop. 200,000), capital of the province. The town possesses one of the greatest tourist attractions in Spain, the *Alhambra Palace*.

In A.D. 711 the town was taken by the Moors. They built a fortress, where the *Alhambra* now stands. When the Caliphate of Cordoba was dissolved, the town's Arabic governor founded an independent dynasty. In 1492 *Ferdinand and Isabella* recaptured the city. The Christian rulers displayed their taste in great buildings (the cathedral and the palace of Charles V).

Granada is beautifully situated on the R. *Genil*, protected by mountains: in the S. by the *Alhambra* ridge, and in the N. by the *Albaicin*, where a large colony of gipsies live in caves—complete with electric light and telephones! Make a trip there and perhaps see them dancing in their colourful costumes.

Places of Interest:

The *Alhambra* is the most interesting place in Granada. From the *Plaza Nueva* you ascend the street, the *Cuesta de Comerez*, to the main entrance, the *Puerta de las Grandas*. To the r., on the *Monte Mauror* are the ruins of the 13th-c. fortress with the towers of *Berjemas*. Walkers can follow the steep *Cuesta Empedrada*. Turn to the l. and go through the *Puerta de la Justicia* and then

Granada with the Alhambra on the right and the snow-capped peaks of the Sierra Nevada in the distance

through a corridor to the *Puerta del Vino*. Motorists use the carriage road. Entrance tickets can be bought in the *palace of Charles V*. A visit to the *Alhambra* includes:

The *Alcazaba*, the ruins of the oldest Arab fortress, begun under Mohammed I (9th c.) with towers of the 13th c. There is a wonderful view from the *Vela tower*. Next:

The *Alhambra palace*, also called the *Alcazar* or the *Palacio Arabe* (14th c.). The exterior is sober, but inside the architecture and the rich decoration are overwhelming. See the former council-chamber, the *Mexuar*, now converted into a chapel, and the *Patio del Mexuar*, through which you come into the *Myrtle Court*, or *Patio de los Arrayanes*. It is 16 ft. long and 75 ft. wide. In the court is a pool, surrounded by a myrtle hedge. At the N. end is the *Comares Tower* (140 ft), containing the *Sala de los Embajadores*, 35 by 35 ft., and 40 ft. high, the former throne-room. The dome is constructed in larch. Go from the Comares Tower along the l. side of the Myrtle Court, turn l. through the *Sala de los Mozarabes* to the famous *Lion Court*, or *Patio de los Leones*, 90 ft. by 55 ft., surrounded by 124 pillars. In the centre is the *lion fountain*, with 12 granite lions. As, according to the Koran, Arabs are not allowed to represent living creatures in their art, the lions are stylized. The *lion court* used to be the centre, around which the royal quarters and the harem were grouped. From the S. side of the court you come into the *Abencerage room*, so-called after a noble family, with a 12-sided fountain and a richly decorated vaulted ceiling. On the E. side is the king's room, *Sala de los Reyes*, with 7 divisions, all equally decorated. From the E. side of the court,

you come into the *two sisters' room*, the *Sala de las Dos Hermanas*, which together with the adjacent room is supposed to have been the women's winter residence. The ornamentation in these rooms is particularly beautiful. We go on to the *Sala de los Ajimeces* (bay windows). In the centre of the wall is a bay, the so-called *Mirador de Daraxa*. One looks on to the *Patio de Daraxa*. We now go up into the gallery along the *Patio de Daraxa*, through some of the chambers. From the top story of the *Torre del Peinador* (to the r., after the emperor's and the queen's rooms) there is a magnificent view, e.g. over the *Generalife* (see below). Return to the galleries, descend the stairs to the *Patio de la Reja* and from here enter the idyllic *Patio de Daraxa*. You can now come into the underground rooms, e.g. *Sala de los Secretos*. We also visit the old baths (rooms for women and children respectively). Come up into the *Myrtle Court* and now visit

The *palace of Charles V*, still incomplete. You see the immense outer walls and the impressive pillared court, intended for bull-fights. Within the palace is the *Alhambra museum*, including the famous vase, *el jarra de la Alhambra* (1320), 4 ft. high, decorated with coloured enamel which Ferdinand and Isabella found filled with gold coins in 1492.

S. of Charles V's palace is the church of *Santa Maria* (16th c.). A visit to Alhambra should be completed by a tour through the gardens, round the fortification walls and into the towers.

The Lion Court in the Alhambra

Part of the Generalife gardens

The *Generalife* was the Moorish king's summer residence, completed in 1319. The name comes from the Arabic: *Djarnat el Arif* (lovely gardens). Through the beautiful, cool cyprus avenue, you reach the main entrance (16th c.). We enter a large *Patio* and go on into the *Sala de los Marqueses* and the *Sala de los Reyes*. Between these is a little *Patio* with a tree, which is said to have been planted by the Moors. Go up over the terraces to the look-out tower (*Mirador*, 1836).

The *cathedral*, *Santa Maria de la Encarnacion*, is regarded as the victory monument of Christianity in Spain. It was begun in 1523, and consecrated in 1561. Its style is Gothic and Renaissance (Plateresque). The W. façade dates from 1667. The *Puerta del Perdon* is the most interesting porch (1537).

The *Capilla Real* is contiguous with the cathedral. Its style is late-Gothic. *Ferdinand and Isabella* and other Spanish kings and queens are buried here.

Albaicin is the picturesque quarter, lying between *Alhambra* and *Sacro Monte*. It is enclosed by a Moorish wall. There is a good view over the *Alhambra* and the *Generalif* from the terrace of *San Nicolas* church, especially at sunset.

Tourist Office: Casa de Cos Tiros.

🏨 Alhambra Palace (L.), near Alhambra. Victoria, Puerta Real 3. 🏨 Parador Nacional de San Francisco, near Alhambra. Inglaterra, Cetti-Merie 4. 🏨 La Perla, Reyes Catolicos 2. Hotel Cantabrico, Navos 26.

△ 6 km E. of the town on the road to *Mulhacen* (by the restaurant).

🚌 (1) Algeciras. (2) Malaga. (3) Cordoba. (4) Madrid. (5) Murcia. (6) Almeria.

🚋 (1) Cordoba. (2) Sevilla. (3) Malaga. (4) Murcia.

Tour 10: Granada—Murcia—Alicante. A: through the mountains (368 km). B: along the coast (491 km)

Both the tours described are very beautiful, but the road via *Guadix-Baza* (A) is better developed and considerably shorter than that via *Almeria* (B).

A: The Mountain Route

We drive out along the *Via de Colon, Acera de San Ildefonso* and *Real de Cartuja*. At the church we turn sharply to the r., and then again to the r. along the *Carretera de Murcia* (N342), which winds up the mountain. From one of the bends there is a glorious view over the town and the *Alhambra*. The road follows the range of the *Sierra Harana*. From the pass of *Puerta de la Mora* (4664 ft.) you can see the snow-capped 11,000-ft. peaks of the *Sierra Nevada*.

Typical cave-dwellings near Guadix

About 20 km further on we enter a district where the bright red earth is cleft by fissures, apparently caused by erosion. Here are numerous cave-dwellings. The total effect of the landscape is very strange. In a suburb of *Guadix* there are many cave-dwellings. The *cathedral* (13th c.) is built on the site of a mosque. The mountain road continues to

BAZA (107 km; 2827 ft.), a very old town where there are ruins of an old Moorish fortress. The road continues through mountainous country to *Velez Rubio*, a pretty little town. Nearby are some caves with prehistoric wall-paintings. After a small ascent we come to

PUERTO LUMBRERAS (204 km; see below).

B: The Coastal Route

We leave Granada along the *Reyes Catolicos, Avenida Jose Antonio* and *Carretera de Genil*, cross the bridge and continue along N323. After *Armilla* there is a good view back over *Granada*. We drive through olive-groves over the pass of *Puerto del Suspiro del Moro* and descend into a valley. From *Beznar* there is a 'short cut' to *Almeria* via *Orjiva*—but it is only shorter in distance, not in time. The scenery is beautiful but the road is not good. The main road continues to

MOTRIL (72 km; pop. 23,000). The town is beautifully situated at the foot of the *Sierra la Contraviesa* (a continuation of the *Sierra Nevada*), only 3 km from the sea.

As we continue along the coast-road (N340), the climate is so mild that we find orange- and lemon-groves, date-palms, banana-palms and sugar-cane. We pass through some small fishing villages. After *Adra*, a little port, the road leaves the coast and runs through a coastal plain to the *Golfo de Almeria*.

ALMERIA (185 km; pop. 90,000) was founded by the Phoenicians, and grew under the Arabs. It is now an important port, with a mild climate, suitable for winter holidays. See the 16th-c. *cathedral* with the lovely Renaissance front. It was originally fortified. The ruined Moorish fortress, the *Alcazaba*, has a Gothic tower (15th c.). The old mosque is also interesting. Near the *Alcazaba* is the fortress of *San Cristobal*, with its *chapel*, erected by the Templars (12th c.). From the terrace is a magnificent view over the bay.

Tourist Office: Av. Gen. Franco 115.
🚂 (1) Madrid. (2) Granada. (3) Cordoba. (4) Murcia.
🚌 (1) Malaga. (2) Murcia.
🏨 Simon, Avenida Generalisimo 38. 🏨 Andalucia, Calle del General Sliquet 17.
▲ In *Alhama de Almeria* (8 km).

We now go N., again passing some cave-dwellings; we drive under two aqueducts and then leave the orange-groves for a more barren landscape; but when we have crossed the *R. Valdelecho*, the district is once again fertile. There is a stretch of rough road. Just before *Vera* (interesting church) we see a colossal figure of *San Cleophas* on a rock.

PUERTO LUMBRERAS (327 km; 1514 ft.). On the far side of the town there is an *Alberque* (🏨).

Lorca on the *R. Guadalatin* has an old quarter with some attractive old mansions and a ruined fortress (good view). The road to *Murcia* is lined by palm-trees.

MURCIA (408 km; pop. 240,000), the provincial capital, lies in a fertile plain, which is artificially drained ('*huertas*'). The *cathedral* is interesting (reconstructed in the 18th c.). From the tower there is a fine view over the town, the '*huertas*' and the mountains.

Palm trees in the forest of Elche

🏨 Reina Victoria, Explanada Arenal 1.
🏨 Internacional, Calle Jose Antonio Ponzos 10.

▲ (1) Colegio Mayor Ruiz de Alda, Huerto de Capuchinos (Zarandona). (2) 5 km outside Murcia in La Alberca: Albergue del Frente de Juventudes.
🚂 (1) Madrid. (2) Almeria. (3) Granada. (4) Alicante. (5) Cartagena.
🚌 (1) Alicante. (2) Granada. (3) Almeria.

We leave *Murcia* by N340 beside the *R. Segura*, passing the park and the bull-ring. At the little village of *Monteagudo* there are the ruins of an old Moorish fort and a colossal statue of Christ (45 ft., view). We now cross the huge *Huerta*, the fertile plain with lemons, oranges, vines and palms. It is very hot here in summer. In *Orihuela* there is a large seminary and a 15th-c. cathedral. The palms become more numerous and, on the r., we soon see

ELCHE (466 km; pop. 54,000), famous for its palm forest, the only one in Europe. The flat-roofed, white

houses against the background of palms give the impression of being in an African oasis. The palm forest is divided into squares by the artificial canals, necessary to supply sufficient water. A visit to the forest will take a few hours; there are 200,000 palms, up to 130 ft. high, mostly date palms. Try iced dates and lemonade as a refresher before continuing to

ALICANTE (491 km; see tour 11).

Tour 11: Alicante—Valencia (184 km)

ALICANTE (pop. 121,000), founded by the Romans, is pleasantly situated on a natural harbour, very important for the export of raisins, almonds, wine, olive-oil, etc. In the background on a hill is the huge ruined fortress of *Santa Barbara*. Otherwise the town has little of interest. The fact that there are so many tourists is due to the climate, which is very mild, even in winter; Alicante is also inexpensive.

Tourist Office: Explanada de España 2.

🏨 Gran Hotel, Navas 43. 🏨 Victoria, Calle de San Fernando 19. Pallas, Calle de Cervantes 5. 🏨 Pastor, Calle de San Fernando 42. Garcia, Calle de Castano 5.

▲ Hogar San Fernando, Calderon de la Barca 28.

△ By the *Bay of San Juan*, 10 km NE.

🚌 (1) Murcia. (2) Madrid. (3) Valencia.

🚏 (1) Valencia. (2) Murcia.

The route along the coast to *Valencia* (N332) is particularly beautiful. There are

The Cuarte Gate at Valencia

good beaches on the northern outskirts of *Alicante*. We drive past the small fortified town of *Villajoyosa* and come to another beach (△, restaurant).

Benidorm is a glorious little holiday resort beautifully situated and with two good beaches. Just before *Altea* you see ahead the *Peñon de Ifach*, which reminds one a little of the rock of *Gibraltar*. The district is now mountainous and the road runs through a few tunnels to *Venta la Canere*; possible detour to *Punta de Ifach* (🏨, beautiful scenery).

The main road leaves the coast for a while and goes through *Gata* and *Ondara* (from here you can make a detour to the fishing harbour of *Denia*).

Gandia is a cosy little town, at the foot of the *Sierra de Gandia*. The church and the home of the *Borgias* (small museum) are interesting. Their magnificent castle is inland at *Jativa* (60 km). The main crop here is rice. Much rice is eaten in Spain and most of it is cultivated in *Valencia*. We pass *Cullera* (pilgrim church) and come to *Sueca*, where the road forks (r.) to *El Perello* on the small isthmus between the fresh-water lake, *Albufera*, and the *Mediterranean*.

VALENCIA (184 km; pop. 610,000), founded by the Ancient Greeks, was later taken over by the Carthaginians and the Romans. In the 5th c. it was conquered by the Visigoths, and 300 years later by the Moors, who remained until the arrival of the Christians in 1094; however, the Moors returned, and held the town until 1238.

It is the third largest town in Spain with a lively Southern character. It is the seat of an archbishop, a university town and an important marketing town for the *Huerta's* produce of raisins, wine, rice, olive-oil, oranges etc. It exports through the port of *El Grao*.

There is not very much to interest tourists, although the life in the town in itself is an attraction, but here are a few things you should see (the figures in square brackets refer to the plan):

The *cathedral* [1], *La Seo*, was begun in 1262. On the same site had stood a Roman temple, a Visigothic church and a Moorish mosque! It contains the Holy Grail sought by King Arthur's Knights of the Round Table. There is a good view from the tower (200 ft.). Every Thursday at noon peasants meet in front of the porch, *Puerta de los*

The Exchange, La Lonja, at Valencia

Apostoles, as they have done since Moorish times, to settle disagreements concerning the watering of their plots on the *Huerta*. The church houses some precious works of art, e.g. by *Goya*. A bridge connects the cathedral with the bishop's palace. See the lovely court.

Torres de Serranos [2] is the old N. town-gate, originally erected 1393–8, later reconstructed (tower, view).

Colegio del Patriarca [3] (16th c. Women not admitted). See the fine court, framed by arcades. There are some wonderful Flemish tapestries in the chapel. In the rector's quarters on the 1st floor there is a fine art collection, e.g. works by El Greco, Morales, Ribalta and Van der Weyden. Contiguous with the *Colegio* is the church of *Corpus Christi* (1586) with a painting of the last supper by Ribalta (1606).

Lonja de la Seda [4] is the old silk exchange (1482–98) with a fine façade. The ceiling in the main hall is supported by elaborate spiral pillars. From here one can enter the tower (144 steps).

Museo de Bellas Artes [5] contains 2000 paintings, e.g. works by Goya, Ribalta, Ribera, El Greco and Velazquez.

Torres de Cuarte [6] (1440–90), scarred by bullets in the Napoleonic wars, is reached through the *Calle de Caballeros* and the *Calle de Cuarte*. Nearby is the *Botanical Gardens* with many subtropical plants.

Tourist Office: Town hall (gd. floor).

🏨 Excelsior, Calle de Hermanas Chabas 5. 🏨 Hotel Londres, Barcelonina 1. Hotel La Marcelina, Plaza Levante 76 (famous for its 'paella'). Hotel Metropol, Jativa 23. 🏨 Hotel España, Plaza del Candillo 20. Hotel Avenida, Plaza del Candillo 2.

🔺 Colegio Menor Rey D. Jaime, Avenida del Puerto 28.

△ S. of *Valencia* by the beach, *Playa de Nazaret*.

🚂 (1) Madrid. (2) Alicante. (3) Tarragona–Barcelona.

🚌 (1) Madrid. (2) Alicante. (3) Seville.

⚓ Palma de Mallorco.

✈ (1) Madrid. (2) Barcelona. (3) Seville. (4) Palma de Mallorca. Also international routes.

Tour 12: Valencia—Tarragona—Barcelona (360 km)

Leaving *Valencia*, we pass the *Torres de Serranos* (see map [2], p. 49), and cross the *R. Turia*. Follow the tram-lines until you join N340. Here N. of the town we are still in the *Huerta*, the artificially irrigated plain. After driving 20 km we see *Sagunto*, where there is *a Roman theatre* and a *Carthagenian fort* on a ridge above the town (view). On the l. is the *Sierra de Espadon* (4553 ft.). In *Almenara James I of Aragon* defeated the Moors (1238), after which Valencia became Christian. Near *Nules* is the little spa, *Villavieja*, with some good spa hotels. In *Villareal* is an old church with an unusual octangular tower.

A view over Sagunto, with the Roman amphitheatre on the right and the medieval fortifications on the hillside to the left

CASTELLON DE LA PLANA (67 km; pop. 55,000) is an important market town, with a port (some adequate hotels).

Coming out of *Castellon*, we see on the l. the mountain summit, *Peña Golosa* (5892 ft.). There is an excellent bathing-beach near *Benicasim* and in *Alcala de Chivert* we notice an old ruined fortress and a pretty church. Soon afterwards we make a detour (7 km) to *Peñiscola*, a very ancient little fortress-town on a rocky peninsula. We continue along the coast to *Benicarlo*, with its old castle, lovely church, and excellent *Albergue* (🏠, swimming-pool). We drive along N340 to the little fishing town of

VINAROZ (152 km). From here N232 leads to *Zaragoza* (235 km). We continue by the coast-road which soon turns inland to

TORTOSA (196 km), an old town on the *R. Ebro*, with a *cathedral* (1347, Moorish tower, cloister) and other interesting churches,

the remains of an old wall and many fine mansions. We continue down the l. bank of the river back to the coast, where we look out over the Ebro delta with the *Isla de Gracia*. In *Hospitalet del Infante*, with its old pilgrims' hospital, there is a camping place (△). We enter the fertile district of *Campo de Tarragona*, with its extensive vineyards.

TARRAGONA (288 km; pop. 47,000), capital of the Catalan province of *Tarragona*, is an important wine-producing town. There was a prehistoric settlement here in the 5th–3rd c. B.C. It later became an important Roman centre with almost 1,000,000 inhabitants. Many relics of that period have survived the troubled times which followed.

Places of Interest:

The *town hall* (*Ayuntamiento* or *Casa Consistorial*) is in the *Plaza de Jose Antonio*, where the Roman 'Circus' (show-place) used to be. In the town hall is the *Archaeological Museum of Tarragona Province*, one of the most interesting in Spain, containing Roman sculptures and mosaics. NB: the museum is to be moved to a new building near the *Palacio de Augusto* (see below).

The *prehistoric–Roman town walls*. Take a walk along the *Paseo Arqueologica* and see the remains of the ancient wall, *Murallas Ciclopeas*. It is 10–30 ft. high and 3 km long.

The *cathedral* was begun in 1278 in Romanesque style and later completed in Gothic. The interior is very impressive, and the *high-altar* particularly beautiful. The *cloister* with 260 pillars is one of the loveliest in Spain. There is a little museum.

The Cathedral of Tarragona

The Roman aqueduct north of Tarragona | *The triumphal arch, Arco de Bara*

The *Palacio de Augusto*, or *Torreon de Pilatus*, is the Roman Praetorium, the governor's palace, erected in the 1st c. A.D., and destroyed by the French in 1811. Next door is the building which is to house the *Archaeological Museum*.

The *Roman Amphitheatre* dates from the time of *Emperor Augustus*. It was excavated in 1952.

The *Necropolis* is an old Christian churchyard, lying on the W. edge of the town (in the grounds of a tobacco factory). There is an adjoining museum.

The *Aqueduct*, 4 km NW. of *Tarragona*, is called 'The Devil's Bridge', *El Puente del Diablo* (700 ft. long).

Tourist Office: Rambla del Generalisimo 50.

🏨 Europa, Rambla del Generalisimo 60. Paris, Rambla de San Carlos 6. 🏨 Internacional, Calle del Conde de Rius 17.

△ La Fabrega, in *Castelltersoll* (on the road to *Barcelona*).

🚌 (1) Barcelona. (2) Zaragoza–Madrid. (3) Valencia.

There are also many Roman relics outside *Tarragona*. We continue along N340, the *Carretera a Barcelona*, and after about 5 km turn off to the *Torre de los Escipiones*, a Roman mausoleum of the 1st c. A.D.

We drive through fertile landscape to *Torredembarra* and soon afterwards we glimpse the *Arco de Bara*, a Roman triumphal arch (2nd c. A.D., 40 ft. high).

In *Vendrell* the road forks. N340 goes inland via *Villafranca del Panades* (from here you could make a detour to *Montserrat*, see tour 14). The charming coast road is 3 km longer and runs through *Villanueva y Geltru* (interesting museum—El Greco), *Sitges*, a delightful seaside resort with many hotels (*Tourist Office:* San Pablo 4), and *Castelldefels*, another resort popular with the people of **BARCELONA** (360 km; see p. 22).

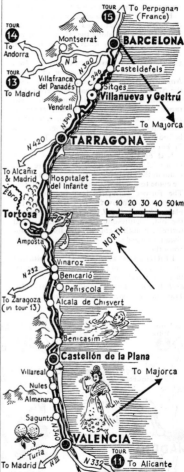

51

Tour 13: Barcelona—Zaragoza—Madrid (630 km)

This tour is the quickest route between Spain's two largest cities. If you have a little more time, we would suggest a detour (50 km longer) via *Tarragona* (tour 12) and *Alcañiz*.

From the *Plaza Cataluña* we drive along the *Paseo de Gracia* to the *Plaza de la Victoria*, and then to the l. along the *Av. del Generalisimo Franco*, which leads out on to N II. After a while we cross the impressive *Llobregat Bridge* to the cross-roads, *Cuatro Caminos*.

Martorell lies at the junction of the *R. Noya* with the *R. Llobregat*. The bridge over the *Noya* is supposed to have been erected by *Hannibal* (218 B.C.). The triumphal arch was raised in memory of his father, *Hamilcar Barca*. Make a detour to the mountain Monastery of *Montserrat* (see p. 54) just before the village of *Collbato* (r.). The extra 21 km are well worth while.

N II continues with many curves to the industrial town of *Igualada*. We are now again in the lovely *Noya* valley. After a tunnel we come to *Cervera*, dominated by its church. The former *university* is now used as a museum. We follow the *R. Cervera* over the plain, *Llano de Urgel*, and see in the distance the old, picturesque town *Bellpuig* (ruined fortress, beautiful church, and former Franciscan monastery with 16th-c. cloister). We cross the *R. Segre* to

LERIDA (160 km; pop. 41,500), situated on a ridge. This old episcopal town has picturesque streets and an old cathedral (*Catedral Antigua*—13th c.), built in Romanesque-Transitional style. The *new cathedral*, the

The cloister at Poblet

bishop's palace, the *town hall* and the *old fort* are also interesting. *Excursion:* it is a long way (54 km) to the monastery of *Poblet*, but a visit is worth while; it is one of the most interesting of Spanish monasteries (12th c. and later).

🏛 Palacio, Porticos Bajos 11. 🏛 Agramunt. Plaza de España 20.

🚌 (1) Barcelona. (2) Zaragoza. (3) Poblet–Parragona.

🚍 (1) Barcelona. (2) Zaragoza. (3) Seo de Urgel.

We continue through *Alcarraz* to the idyllically situated town of *Fraga*. The road now crosses the arid plateau of *Los Monegros* through *Bujaraloz*. The landscape is desolate. We descend into the *Ebro valley*, following the river to

ZARAGOZA (304 km; pop. 300,000), the provincial capital. The town lies where the *Huerva* and the *Gallego* flow into the *Ebro*, in the middle of a fertile, artificially irrigated plain. A prehistoric settlement, it was called by the Romans *Caesar-Augustae*, from which its name derives. It later came under Visigothic and Moorish rule. Under Alfonso I of Aragon, *Zaragoza* became the capital of *Aragon*, but it lost that position under

Ferdinand and Isabella. The town gained fame during the Spanish war of liberation against the French (1808–9), when half the inhabitants died, either from war wounds, sickness or starvation. It is a leading university town. Town life centres around the *Plaza de España* and the main thoroughfares, *Calle del Coso* and *Paseo de la Independencia*, stretching to the *Plaza de Aragon*. The four most interesting buildings in *Zaragoza* are all near the *Ebro:*

The church of Nuestra Señora del Pilar and the old stone bridge over the Ebro at Zaragoza

La Seo, the cathedral, in the *Plaza de la Seo* (at the end of the Plaza del Pilar), was begun in the 12th c. and finished in the 17th c., although the main porch dates from 1795. The long period of construction has meant that all the changing styles from Romanesque and Moorish to Baroque are represented. Notice the attractive lattice in the chancel and the Gothic *choir-stalls*. In the *Capilla Mayor* there is a lovely alabaster altar-piece by a German master (1473–7). There is a small museum with some Flemish tapestries (15th c. and later).

La Lonja is the Renaissance style exchange (1551). Next door is the modern town hall. Notice the 15th-c. 7-arched bridge, *Puenta de Piedra* (good view from other side).

Go past the town hall to the new cathedral of *Nuestra Señora del Pilar*, the object of many pilgrimages, especially in connection with the ‘*Fiesta de la Raza*’ (12th Oct.), in memory of the discovery of America. The huge building was erected in the 17th c. It has 10 domes, two large towers and measures 400 by 200 ft. The 16th-c. Gothic alabaster *altar-piece* is its most interesting feature.

Zaragoza's Museum in the *Plaza de Jose Antonio* contains ethnographical, archaeological and art collections.

Tourist Office: Plaza de Sas 7.

🏨 Gran Hotel, Calle de Costa 5 (L.). Goya, Calle de Requete Aragones 5. 🏨 Centenario, Calle de Bruil 2. Hotel Lafuente, Valenzuela 73. 🏨 Eriente, Calle de Coso 11.

▲ Residencia Universitaria ‘Matlas Montero’, Calvo Sotelo 17.

🚌 (1) On main line Madrid–Barcelona. (2) Lerida.

🚋 Lerida.

We leave *Zaragoza*, climbing the *La Muela* mountains with the *Sierra de Muela* (2034 ft.), and then descend to the lowlands of *Llano de Plasencia*. The road climbs again and crosses the passes of *Puerto de Morata* (2301 ft.), *Puerto del Frasno* (2535 ft.) and *Puerto de Cavero* (2486 ft.) to

CALATAYUD (390 km; 1696 ft.), dominated by the ruins of the Moorish fort, *Kalat*. In the mountains above the town are some deserted cave-dwellings. There are several interesting churches and on the outskirts (NE. near the *R. Jalon*) are the ruins of a Celtic town, *Bilbilis*.

Now we enter a wine-district, go past *Ateca* (Moorish town wall, 9th-c. castle), through a tunnel and wind down to

ALHAMA DE ARAGON, where the *R. Jalon* flows through an impressive gorge. Make a detour to the Cistercian monastery of *Piedra* (17 km), situated in pleasant countryside.

We follow the river past more deserted caves. The road is very winding. We emerge from a tunnel and see, to the r., the town of *Medinaceli* with its Roman ruins (*Albergue* 🏨). The road ascends steeply to *Alcolea del Pinar* (3916 ft.).

The ruins of the old monastery of Piedra

In *Guadalajara* there are many old mansions and churches. We pass through Cervantes’ birth-place, *Alcala de Henares*, where there is a fine ruined University and a 16th-c. inn, and *Torrejon de Ardoz*, past the airport, *Barajas*, to

MADRID (630 km ; see p. 18).

Tour 14: Barcelona—Montserrat—Andorra (245 km)

A visit to the Lilliputian semi-independent republic of *Andorra* (see *Gateway Guide to France*, p. 48) is well worth including in a tour of Spain. In this tour we shall visit the mountain of *Montserrat* with its impressive monastery.

For the way out of Barcelona see tour 13, which we follow to *Martorell*. Just before the village of *Collbato*, we turn off to the r. (sign-post: Manresa–Montserrat). The road winds up the mountain, skirting a valley with saltpetre mines, crosses a high-level bridge over the *R. Llobregat*, and continues through *Monistrol*, from which there is a rack-railway up to *Montserrat* (35–40 min.). The road ascends very steeply, but there is a good asphalt surface. One has a wonderful view over the valley. We pass the *peñascos*, tower-like rock formations, and can see the aerial railway rising high above us, leading to the highest peak, *San Jeronimo*. To the l. of it are the two rocks, *Roca de Patricia* and *Roca de las Once* (Eleven Apostles' Rock). We pass Hotel Colonia Puig (🏨) and the road, which leads to *Manresa* (pop. 45,000; interesting churches) and soon reach the

MONASTERIO DE MONTSERRAT (60 km; 2343 ft.). In 880 a hermitage was built on the spot, where the *Virgin Mary* was said to have appeared. This legend inspired *Wagner* to write 'Parcifal'. *Pope Benedict XIII* erected a monastery on the site (1410). It was subsequently extended and acquired great wealth, which to a large extent was lost in later years. Since the 14th c. there has been a choir school of the best voices in the country in the monastery, whose pupils sing thanksgiving hymns each morning at 6 and at evening mass. Most pilgrims come to Montserrat on the 27th April and the 8th Sept., especially young married couples, who come to ask the Virgin Mary for a blessing upon their marriage, and many Catalans come here to be married. One of the attractions is the wooden figure of the Virgin and Child, 'The black Virgin' (*Moreneta*). There are many museums here: the Bible museum, an Egyptological collection, a prehistoric collection, a natural history museum and an art gallery. The large library is also interesting.

The mountain is 22 km long and rises almost perpendicularly out of the plain above the *R. Llobregat*. We recommend these excursions:

Turo de San Jeronimo (4033 ft.). Take the aerial railway from the restaurant 'Santa Cecilia' on the road to *Manresa* (passed on the way to Andorra). It takes 10 min. from the mountain station to the summit. There is a magnificent view over the *Pyrenees, Barcelona* and in clear weather to *Majorca*. From the hermitage, *San Jeronimo*, near the mountain station one can walk back to

San Juan, from where there is a ½-km long rack-railway down again to the monastery. Round about San Juan are ruins of previous hermitages.

The *Grotto of the Black Virgin*, where, according to legend, the Moors found the miraculous statue, which caused the monastery to be built. A 17th-c. chapel stands here.

The mountain monastery of Montserrat

Capilla de San Miguel is on the road to *Collbato* (25 min.). You can combine it with a trip to the look-out tower, *Mirador*.

An excursion to Montserrat from Barcelona:
🚌 From the *Plaza de la Universidad*. Depart 9 a.m., return 6.30 p.m.
🚃 (with rack-railway). From the *Plaza de Cataluña*, 8.15, 10.15, 2.15. Sundays, also 6.15 a.m.
🏨 *Monasterio*, near the monastery. 🏨 *Colonia Puig*, on the way to Monistrol. 🏨 *Marcet*, near Colonia Puig.

You can also spend the night in the monastery cells if you apply to the *Despacho de Aposentos* (no service; men only).

We leave *Montserrat* and turn off to the l. past the restaurant of Santa Cecilia. On the r. is the road to *Manresa*. We keep to the l. and come out on road N II, which we follow for 10 km beyond *Igualada*, where we turn to the r. towards *Pons*, passing some small towns, with old fortresses, and see the *Pyrenees* towering in the distance.

From *Pons* the road follows the *R. Segre* through beautiful country, and then through the gorge of *Graho de la Grande*, where a dam is under construction. After crossing a more open area, we come to another still more impressive gorge, *Garganta de Orgaña*. We cross the *Segre* and pass some more small towns to

SEO DE URGEL (224 km; 2275 ft.; pop. 7000), the seat of the bishop, who, with the President of France, is co-ruler of *Andorra*. The *cathedral* was founded in the 11th c., but has been rebuilt several times since. The tower on the ridge above the town is the *Torre Solsona*. From 'La Seo', as the town is called locally, there are direct roads to *Puigcerda* and *Perpignan*.

The frontier control is a little N. of *Seo de Urgel*. At present no visa is necessary for entry into *Andorra*. After the frontier, we enter more mountainous country. We drive through the *Valira* valley and soon reach the capital

ANDORRA LA VELLA (245 km; 3344 ft.; see *Gateway Guide to France*, p. 48).

Tour 15: Barcelona—Perpignan (France).
A: direct (191 km). B: via the Costa Brava (310 km)

We recommend the coast road, although it is considerably longer and parts of it are in bad condition. The 'Costa Brava' is now one of Spain's principal summer resorts. But for those who do not have much time we describe the shorter route also.

(See also: *Gateway guide to the Costa Brava, Majorca and Ibiza*.)

A: Via Gerona

We leave *Barcelona* by the *Calle de Almogavares* bringing you out on to road N II (see plan p. 23).

The road runs along the coast through *Badalona* and *Mongat* (castle). The coast here is called the *Costa Levantina*—good bathing. The first largish town is *Mataro* (32,000). A little later we pass a camping place, 'La Bovila', and the little resort of *Caldetas*, with

hot springs. Just beyond is *Arenys de Mar*, a small harbour town with a good beach. The coast becomes rocky, but in *Canet de Mar* the sand beaches return. *San Pol* is pleasantly situated between road and beach. We top a small ridge (view) and descend again to the shore.

After *Pineda* the road forks. The coast road continues along the *Costa Brava* (see below) and the main road turns inland. We follow the main road over a spur of the *Sierra Montnegre*, from which there are many wonderful views over the coast. In *Caldas de Malavella* (△) the hot springs (95° F.) were known by the Romans. *Caldas* is ca. 3 km off the road to the r. towards *San Feliu de Quixols*. Through pine-forests and groves of cork-oak we come to the provincial capital,

GERONA (100 km; pop. 45,000). The

The old fortress at Tossa del Mar

cathedral, with a lovely inner cloister and the monastery church, *San Feliu*, are interesting, and the old quarter is very picturesque.

Tourist Office: Ciudadanos 12.

🏨 Peninsular, Calle del General Primo de Rivera 3. Hotel Italianos, Ciudadanos 16. ♨ Centro, Calle de Ciudadanos 4.—△.

🚂 On main line Barcelona–Perpignan.

🚌 (1) Barcelona. (2) Lloret. (3) Palafrugell–Palamos.

A side road leads down to the 'Costa Brava'.

We pass *Sarria* and continue through very hilly country, cross the *R. Fluvia* and then the *R. Manol* and come out into flat country, with vineyards known as the *Ampurdan*.

Figueras is dominated by the 18th-c. castle, *Castillo de San Fernando*, a massive pentagonal building. From here you can descend to the northern section of the 'Costa Brava', or make the detour through *Port Bou* to *Perpignan*.

The main road continues to the frontier town of *La Junquera* (Spanish frontier post), and then through forests of cork-oak and over the low pass of *Col de Perthus* (945 ft.; French frontier post). The town lies on both sides of the frontier. After some small towns we reach

PERPIGNAN (191 km; pop. 75,000; see *Gateway Guide to France*, p. 49).

B: via the Costa Brava

We follow tour 15A to *Pineda*, and continue along the coast road, which is signposted *Malgrat*. After this town we see ahead the conical mountain, *San Juan*.

BLANES is an idyllic little fishing town, frequented by holiday makers.

🏨 Hotel del Parque. 🏨 Mediterraneo, Paseo del Mar. ♨ Miramar, Plaza de España 56.—△.

We recommend a detour (2 km) to the restaurant at *Santa Cristina* (view). After the next fishing village, *Lloret de Mar* (many hotels), there is another opportunity for a little rest, if you leave the main road, which

runs above the town, and descend to the Hotel Canellas on the coast. The road follows the rocky coastline.

TOSSA DEL MAR is very popular with foreign tourists. The main road skirts the town, but despite the rather awkward drive in, it is worth taking a look at the town. There are ruins of a Roman villa and Moorish walls, and a good bathing-beach.

🏨 Ancora (lovely garden). 🏨 Rovira, Paseo del Mar 12 and La Playa, Paseo del Mar: both with private beaches. Many others.

The road from *Tossa* to *San Feliu de Quixols* is extremely beautiful, but contains no less than 365 sharp corners. We drive round the hill, *Puig de Cadiretas* (1687 ft.) and come upon one magnificent scene after the other.

A view over the rugged coast of the 'Costa Brava'

SAN FELIU DE GUIXOLS is a small port, important for the export of cork, which this district is so rich in, and is perhaps the most popular resort on the 'Costa Brava' with numerous hotels and 'pensions'.

🏨 Murla, Plaza General Mola 48. 🏨 La Noies, Rambla Jos Antonio 10. Residencia Gesoria, Capmany 3.

The best situated hotels are on the N. beach. Here are some:

Playa S'Agaro: 🏨 Hostal de la Gavina (L.).

Playa de Aro: 🏨 Costa Brava (situated high). ♨ Miramar. A good restaurant, Mare Nostrum (to the r. of Hotel Rancho Suizo).

A little further N. is the small town of *Calonge* with a pleasant hotel: 🏨 San Jorge. △ Near the restaurant of Torre Valentina. This stretch of the coast is equally beautiful and there are many excellent hotels.

PALAMOS, another cork exporting town, is wonderfully situated and attracts many tourists. (Many hotels, △.)

PALAFRUGELL is still partially surrounded by an old town wall, and has a fine church. It is ca. 5 km from the coast, where there are scores of hotels in the small towns of *Calella*, *Llafranch*, *San Sebastian* and *Tamariu*. Near *Tamariu* (△) there are many grottos, accessible by boat. From *Palafrugell* you could turn off to *Gerona* and continue along the better surfaced N II.

We continue along the coast to *Bagur*, which is picturesquely situated opposite *Cape Bagur* (lighthouse). On the coast (side road just before Bagur) is *Aiguablava* (🏛). The road crosses the mouth of the *R. Ter* to *Toroella de Montgri*. From here a side road leads to *Estartit*, from where you can take a boat trip to the *Islas Medias*. We continue along the road to *Figueras* and soon turn off again to *La Escala*, a small fishing village with a beach. From *Escala* one should take a trip to

AMPURIAS, the ruins of the ancient Graeco-Roman town, *Emporion*. The tour goes on past *Vilademat* to *San Pedro Pescador* and later to *Castilla de Ampurias* (interesting church). We make for the coast again—with a possible detour to *Rosas*—at *Cadaques*, a very attractive little fishing town. You could take a boat trip to *Cape Creus*, Spain's most easterly point. The road has a lot of bends. We pass *Llansa* and *San Miguel de Colèra* before reaching the frontier town of

PORT BOU (Spanish frontier post at *Col des Balitres*). We continue through *Cerbère* (French frontier post) to **PERPIGNAN** (310 km; see above).

Tour 16: A Trip Round the Balearic Islands

The *Balearic Islands* lie in the Mediterranean ca. 10 hours' sailing from *Barcelona*. *Palma*, the capital of the largest island, *Majorca*, can be reached in 55 min. by plane from Barcelona. Beside *Majorca*, the islands of *Minorca* and *Ibiza* offer great attractions for holidays.

Majorca

MAJORCA (*Mallorca*) has the best communications with the mainland, and on the island there are several small railways and good roads. The N. part of the island is very mountainous; *Puig Mayor* (4712 ft.) is its highest point. The S. is a fertile lowland, growing olives, almonds, figs, oranges and lemons.

The harbour and Cathedral at Palma

There are several good natural harbours *Palma*, *Soller*, *Pollensa*, *Alcudia* and *Andraitx* and in many places there are small lakes near the coast, 'calas', connected with the sea. These are ideal for water sports. There are also good beaches.

PALMA DE MALLORCA (pop. 152,000), the capital, is an excellent centre for tourists, on account of its good communications.

Places of Interest:

The *cathedral* was begun in 1230, but not completed for 4 centuries. The main front, however, is 19th c. The *high-altar* dates from 1346. The body of king *James II*, who died in 1311, lies in a glass coffin in the *Capilla Mayor*. Huge rose-windows adorn the front. Notice the N. porch, *Almoina*, with its minaret-like tower. The *Miramar* porch with a relief, illustrating the Last Supper, is also lovely. The roof is 150 ft. high and is supported by slim pillars, which divide the interior into a nave and two aisles. In the *treasury* there are some magnificent *objets*

d'art in gold, and a silver statuette of St Peter (relic-shrine). From the terrace there is a lovely view over the Mediterranean.

The church of San Francisco is of the 13th c., in the Gothic style (one side-porch is Baroque), with an especially fine cloister.

La Lonja, the exchange, by the harbour, is 15th-c. Gothic and now contains Majorcas' provincial *museum* (paintings from 15th–17th c.). View from tower.

Castilla de la Almudaina, situated near the cathedral, is an old royal fort. From the court one enters the Gothic *Capilla de Santa Ana*.

Casa Consistorial, the town hall, contains a smaller town museum.

Castilla de Bellver lies just outside the town (SE.). It is a 13th-c. fort with a fine court, and a remarkable view from the tower.

Excursions from Palma:

(1) **VALLDEMOSA** and **SOLLER** (ca. 130 km). We drive W. along the main road, following the S. coast, pass a little to one side of the *Castillo de Bellver* and drive a short way inland, to return to the coast at *Paguera*. Continue N. to *Andraitx*, unless you prefer to drive via *Puerto de Andraitx* (5 km longer, but more beautiful; 🏛 Camp de Mer. 🏛 Playa). From *Andraitx* we continue N. through hills to the W. coast. At *Banalbufar* the road turns inland to

VALLDEMOSA (69 km). The monastery was founded in 1399, and gained fame in 1838, when *Chopin* stayed there for a while with *Georges Sand*. The Spanish government closed the monastery in 1838. Little remains of the original building. The chapel, built in the form of a cross, dates from the 18th c. There are some fine frescoes on the dome and some good sculpture. The saying goes that any virgin, who sits in the *Prior's chair*, can expect to be married by the end of the year. In the *Sacristy* are some church tapestries embroidered in gold and silver. There is a 17th-c. monastery surgery. Some of the cells are fitted out as a *Chopin–Georges Sand Museum* and contain various manuscripts and objects, which belonged to the famous pair, e.g. a piano which Chopin sent for from Paris, some furniture and a collection of books. There is a beautiful view from the terrace. In conjunction with a visit to the monastery, one can go into the adjacent *Palacio del Rey Sancho* and see Majorcan

A view from the road to Formentor   *The Dragon Caves*

folk-dances, presented by a local group, every Monday, Thursday and Saturday.

We continue along the coast to *Soller* and pass the country house, *Miramar*, built by the Austrian, Archduke Ludwig Salvador (1847–1915), in a fine natural park. *Deya* is pleasantly situated among orange-groves (🏨 Costa d'Or, good view).

SOLLER lies in a valley. 5 km from the town is its port, *Puerta del Soller*, visited by many tourists. 🏨 Esplendido; 🏨 Marina; Costa Brava; Marbella; Miramar, etc. From *Soller* one can climb the island's highest mountain, *Puig Mayor* (4712 ft.). It takes about 6 hours and the view is magnificent. Return to Palma over the *Alfabia* pass, through lovely scenery.

(2) **CAPE FORMENTOR** (ca. 170 km) is the northernmost point of *Majorca*. You drive through *Inca* and come to a landscape with many windmills. Go on through *Alcudia*, where there are remains of a 14th-c. town wall and, nearby, a Roman amphitheatre. Continue around the lovely *Pollensa Bay* and over the hills past the magnificent luxury hotel Formentor (🏨), to the furthest point, 10 km from the hotel. The view is glorious. Return via *Pollensa* and *Campanet* (fascinating stalactite caves).

(3) **MANACOR** and **CUEVAS DEL DRACH** (ca. 125 km). *Manacor* is known for its production of pearls. On the coast to the E. are the magnificent stalactite caves, *Cuevas del Drach* (dragon-caves), with an exciting subterranean lake. The tour through the caves takes 1½ hours. Nearby are some smaller stalactite caves, the *Cuevas del Hams*.

(4) **CUEVAS DE ARTA** (ca. 160 km). You drive via *Manacor*, *San Lorenzo* and *San Servera*. These caves are famous for their unusually long stalactite formations. Nearby is the impressive medieval fortified tower, *Canyamel*.

(5) **CUEVAS DE GENOVA** (6 km NW. of *Palma*) are smaller stalactite caves, which you can visit if you have no time for a longer excursion.

NB. One can make reservations for various bus tours of the island, including the places mentioned above, through travel agencies and hotels. Note that the tour to *Valldemosa* does not run on Sundays, nor the tour to *Cuevas del Drach* on Saturdays.

Tour 17

Tourist Office: Paseo General Franco 38.

Hotels: The best and dearest hotels are on the sea-front. This list is only a sample; there are many more. For a full list apply to a travel agency.

In the town: 🏛 Alhambra, Avenida Antonio Maura 5. 🏨 Catalonia, Massanet 1. ⌂ Balear, Plaza Mayor 31.

By the coast W. of Palma: 🏛 Maricel (L.). Principe Alfonso. 🏨 Calamayor, Costa Azul, Paseo Maritimo, Kursaal, Andrea Doria 2. ⌂ Residencia Hidalgo and San Remo.

SE. of Palma, in San Antonio: 🏨 Oasis.

On the Arenal Beach: 🏛 San Francisco.

Some hotels and 'pensions' outside the capital. (P = pension.)

Portals Nous (12 km W., beautiful situation, beach): 🏛 Bendinat. 🏨 Pinos [P].

Paguera (23 km W., beach, forest): 🏨 Bahia. Playa [P].

Puerto de Pollensa (58 km N., fishing village, beach, beautiful situation, near *Formentor*): 🏛 Uyal. 🏨 Miramar. Sis Pins. Rex [P]. ⌂ Marina.

Puerto de Alcudia (78 km N., beach): 🏨 Del Golf. Marisol. ⌂ Marina [P].

Porto-Cristo (53 km E., near *Cuevas del Drach*): ⌂ Felip. Perello.

⌑ (1) Barcelona. (2) Valencia. (3) Minorca. (4) Ibiza.

✈ (1) Barcelona. (2) Madrid. (3) Valencia. Also international routes.

Minorca

MINORCA (Menorca) is the most Eastern of the Balearic isles, with the towns *Mahon* and *Ciudadela*, not visited by two many tourists. The scenery is beautiful and there are more traces of bygone times than in *Mallorca*. There are boat connections with *Palma* and *Barcelona*. 🏛 Hotel Port Mahon; 🏨 Hotel Xuroy.

Ibiza

IBIZA lies ca. 100 km. SW. of *Majorca*, and is beginning to be discovered by tourists. It is an enchanting little holiday island, still not over-civilized. There is a 12th-c. *cathedral* in the capital, *Ibiza* (⌂ Ibiza).

On the W. coast is the lovely town of *San Antonio Abad*.

🏛 Pa Panit. 🏨 San Antonio. Ses Servines. Playa.

⌑ (1) Barcelona. (2) Valencia. (3) Alicante. (4) Palma.

Tour 17: Madrid—Avila—Salamanca—Lisbon (757 km)

This tour connects the two capitals of the Peninsula by an alternative and more interesting route than the main one further S. through *Merida*.

We leave *Madrid* by N VI to the NW. (see map p. 18) and cross the steep *Guadarrama Pass* (4964 ft., with gradients of 1 in 8 and dangerous bends). At *Villacastin*, with its 16th-c. church and arcaded square, we turn l. along N110 to

AVILA (113 km; 3620 ft.; pop. 26,000) situated by the R. *Adaja* on the high Castilian plateau. Founded by the Romans, the town is extremely interesting historically and was the birth-place of St Theresa.

The old town wall, erected in its present form in 1090–9, is one of the best preserved medieval fortifications in Spain. It has a total length of just over 1½ miles, over 80 'dados' (semicircular towers) and 8 gates. Take a walk along the wall round the old quarter from the *Puerta del Alcazar* and go W. to the *Paseo del Calderon* (a fine view over the Ambles valley), continue to the *Puerta de Santa Teresa*. Behind, in the little square is

the *monastery of Santa Teresa* with a fine Baroque church. Returning to the wall, go on past the *Puerta del Puente* until you come to the little Romanesque church of *San Segundo*, and then along the N. side of the wall; on the l. you will see the little church, *Ermita de San Martin*. You will soon reach the impressive church of *San Vicente*; in style it represents the transition from Romanesque to Gothic. Both the interior and the exterior of the church are interesting. Nearby is the lovely *Puerta de San Vicente*, the NE. gate. Walk down the *Calle del Tostado* to the cathedral of

San Salvador, which was begun in 1091, but not completed until the 15th c. The church was originally fortified; inside are some beautiful mosaic windows and other examples of ecclesiastical art. The treasury and cloisters are worth a visit, and there is a good view from the tower.

San Pedro (12th–13th c.) is another interesting church with a lovely rose window. Along the *Paseo de Santo Tomas* you come to the *monastery of San Tomas* with its Gothic

The old town wall of Avila

church and wonderful cloisters. One could also visit Avila's bull-fighting museum.

🚃 On main lines Madrid–Irun and Madrid–Salamanca.

🚌 Segovia.

🏨 Reina Isabel, Avenida Jose Antonio 7.

🏨 Continental, Plaza de la Catedral 4.

🏨 Jardin, Calle de San Segundo 38.

Leaving *Avila* by the *Puerta del Puente*, we cross the river and continue along N501. After a long descent to the *Tormes valley* we reach the golden sandstone city of

SALAMANCA (212 km; 2623 ft.; pop. 105,000), which lies in a wide plain, almost without trees. It was also founded by the Romans and contains Spain's most famous university.

The *Plaza Mayor* is a good place to start a tour of the town. The square is in the Baroque style of the early 18th c. and is the loveliest in Spain. The building with the spire is the *Casa Consistorial*, and the town hall, the *Ayuntamiento* (1755), is also in the square. Notice the church of *San Martin* (12th c.).

From the square go along the *Rua Mayor* to the cathedral,

Catedral Nueva, begun in 1500 but not completed until 1733. The west porch is particularly beautiful. It is the last great Gothic building in Spain. Near it is the old cathedral,

Catedral Vieja, a Romanesque building of the 12th c. The fine cupola of the *Torre del Gallo* is supposed to date from about 1100. See the huge altar and the *Virgin of La Vega*, a medieval masterpiece in gold and Limoges enamel.

From the cathedral you can continue along the *Rua Mayor* and then turn r. along the *Ribera del Puente* to the old Roman bridge, *Puente Romano*, of which the 15 arches nearest the town are original. Return towards the Catedral Vieja. Not far from it, on the r., is the

University, with a magnificent Plateresque façade (1529). Have a look inside the beautiful courtyard; the staircase leading to the

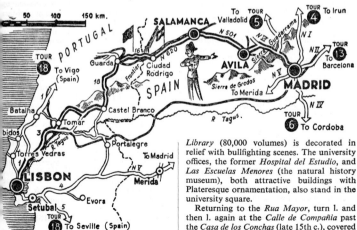

Library (80,000 volumes) is decorated in relief with bullfighting scenes. The university offices, the former *Hospital del Estudio*, and *Las Escuelas Menores* (the natural history museum), both attractive buildings with Plateresque ornamentation, also stand in the university square.

Returning to the *Rua Mayor*, turn l. and then l. again at the *Calle de Compañia* past the *Casa de los Conchas* (late 15th c.), covered in stone shells (r.), to the *Palacio de Monterrey*, a beautiful example of Spanish Renaissance architecture (1538), which has often been copied. If you continue along the street keeping to the l. you will come to the *Colegio del Arzobispo* with an attractive porch and an interesting church.

If you still have time, return the way you came, cross the *Rua Mayor* and come out in the *Calle de San Pablo* opposite the *Dueñas monastery* (1533). A little further on is the church of

San Esteban (1524–1610), with its fine gabled front in the Plateresque style, like a triptych, which is on a par with that of the University. There are some good paintings inside, e.g. *The Martyrdom of St Ursula* (16th c.). Return to the Plaza Mayor along the *Calle de san Pablo*, past the octagonal fortress, *Torre del Clavero* (1480), and (l.) the *Casa de las Salinas* (Plateresque, 16th c.).

🚗 (1) Avila–Madrid. (2) Guarda-Oporto (Portugal).

🚌 (1) Valladolid. (2) Ciudad Rodrigo.

🏨 Grand Hotel, Plaza del Poeta Iglesias 3.

🏨 Pasaje, Plaza Mayor 39.

🏨 Torres, Plaza Mayor 47.

Now we take N620 across the bare plain to **CIUDAD RODRIGO** (301 km), an old fortified town with ruins of a Roman aqueduct and bridge, which contains a very attractive *Parador* in its 14th-c. castle (🏨). The 12th-c. *cathedral* has a carved porch and fine cloisters, and the town is full of beautiful 16th-c. houses built by followers of the 'Conquistadores'. It was after re-capturing it from the French in 1812 that Wellington was made an Earl, Duke of Ciudad Rodrigo, and Marquess of Torres Vedras.

The road from here to the frontier-post at *Fuentes de Onoro* (33 km) is very rough, but on the Portuguese side the surface is excellent, though now the countryside suddenly becomes very hilly and the road has many sharp bends. Soon we reach

GUARDA (387 km; 3370 ft.), perched high above the valley at the NE. extremity of the *Serra da Estrêla*. Founded in 1199 on the site of a Roman settlement, it contains a fine 16th-c. *cathedral* with twisted Manueline pillars.

🚗 (1) Ciudad Rodrigo–Salamanca. (2) Castelo Branco–Lisbon. (3) Coimbra.

🏨 Turismo, Largo de S. Francisco.

From Guarda N18 runs S. through *Covilha* and *Fundão* to

The Cathedral and Roman bridge at Salamanca

CASTELO BRANCO (494 km) with the remarkable 18th-c. *gardens* of the bishop's palace, perhaps the most elaborate and beautiful in Portugal.

🏨 Turismo, Campo da Patria.

We continue by N3 and N241 through *Proenca a Nova* and across the lovely *Zezere valley* to

TOMAR (617 km), dominated by the vast hill-top castle and *Convent of Christ*. Its earliest part is the 12th-c. octagonal *Templars' Church*, the best surviving example in Europe; but the most extraordinary is the early 16th-c. Manueline nave of the *Church of St John the Baptist*, containing the chapter-house with its amazing window, framed by twirled and knotted ropes carved in stone.

Inside the church is the notable *Salome* by Gregorio Lopez. Among the eight cloisters of the Convent the most interesting are those of Henry the Navigator (15th c.) and King John III (16th c.), the latter almost Palladian in style.

Also of exceptional Italian purity in style is the 16th-c. church of *Our Saviour of Conceicão*, halfway down the hill; the 13th-c. *Santa Maria do Olival*, where many of the Knights of the Order of Christ are buried, and *São João Baptista*, with its Gothic pulpit, are also worth seeing.

🏨 Estalagem do Castelo do Bode. 🏨 União, Rua Serpa Pinto 94.

After rejoining N3 at *Torres Novas*, it is not far to *Santarem*, which was once a large Roman colony and had until recently the last bridge over the *R. Tagus*. By the river is the ancient fort called the *Portas do Sol* (fine view), and in the 13th-c. *São João de Alporão* is the beautiful tomb of the Count of Viana. (🏨 Central, Rua Gilherme de Azevêdo 22.)

From here it is only 78 km to **LISBON** (see tour 18).

Tour 18: Vigo—Oporto—Lisbon—Seville (898 km)

You may like to combine a visit to *Portugal* with your holiday in Spain, which is easily done, following tour 17 or this tour, which runs right through the country from N. to S. Many of Portugal's most interesting places lie on this route.

We cross the frontier over the *R. Minho* some 30 km S. of *Vigo*, and continue S. by N13 to

VIANA DO CASTELO (83 km), an attractive seaside town, with a funicular to *Monte de Santa Luzia* (812 ft., fine view). The *Capela dos Malheiros Reimoes* has a charming Baroque façade.

🚆 On main line Vigo–Oporto.

🏨 Grand Hotel Santa Luzia.

From *Espozende* you can make a detour (30 km) to **BRAGA**. Sights: (1) 11th-c. *cathedral*, with its magnificent Baroque organs (1733–7); (2) 14th-c. chapel of *Our Lady of Glory*; (3) Museum of Religious Art; (4) Episcopal Palace (14th–16th c.) with interesting library; (5) many beautiful palaces; (6) mountain shrine of *Bom Jesus do Monte* outside the town (funicular, fine view) with its elaborate Italianate stairway (late 18th c.). From *Braga* you can continue direct along N14 to

OPORTO (153 km; pop. 300,000), the second city of Portugal, originally called *Portucale* from which the country derived its name. A centre of commerce, in particular the port-wine trade, it is dramatically situated on the steep N. bank of the *R. Douro*, dominated by the great two-level bridge and by the *cathedral* (13th–14th c.), with its blue-tiled cloisters and famous solid silver altar. From the terrace is a fine view of the river and the old houses by the waterfront below. Other sights: (1) the 14th-c. *São Francisco*, which is completely encrusted inside with gilded Baroque woodwork; (2) *Santa Clara* (1416), with beautiful Baroque gilt decorations; (3) the 250-ft. *Clerigos Tower* (1748); (4) the 19th-c. *Bourse* or Exchange, with a fantastically vulgar 'Oriental' ballroom; (5) the British *Factory House* (1785); (6) the fine *circular cloister* of the Renaissance church, just across the top bridge (on the l.) in *Vila Nova da Gaia*.

🚆 (1) Vigo. (2) Coimbra–Lisbon. (3) Salamanca.

🏨 Imperio, Praca de Batalha. 🏨 Paris, Rua da Fabrica 27. 🚆 Cominhos de Ferro, Rua da Estação.

Continuing by N1, we pass the *Pousada* (🏨) at *Serem*, and from *Mealhada* a side-road leads to *Buçaco* (12 km), a fantastic 19th-c. Manueline palace, now a luxury hotel (🏨), tacked on to a 17th-c. Carmelite monastery, set in the centre of a beautiful forest, and the site of one of Wellington's first important battles (fine view from top of hill). Shortly we reach the once capital city of

COIMBRA (269 km), with the famous *University* founded in 1307. Its lovely three-sided square, on a hill-top overlooking the town (fine view), contains a magnificent Baroque *library* (1717), a charming small

chapel, and the old *Hall.* Other sights: (1) the Romanesque *Old Cathedral;* (2) *Santa Cruz* (1131) with a double cloister; (3) *Santa Clara* (17th c.), on the other side of the R. *Mondego,* with the silver tomb of St Isabel and a beautiful double cloister.

🚇 (1) On main line Oporto–Lisbon. (2) Guarda.

🏨 Astoria. 🏨 Internacional (both Avenida Navarro). 🏛 Central, Praca 8 de Maio 37.

From here you could make a detour to the fashionable seaside resort of *Figueira da Foz* (46 km).

After leaving *Coimbra,* we pass the ruins of the 12th-c. castle of *Pombal* and *Leiria,* with another great ruined castle, before reaching the magnificent abbey of

BATALHA, with its famous *'Unfinished Chapels',* and founded by King John I in 1388; see also the *founder's chapel* with the tombs of the King and his Queen, Philippa of Lancaster, daughter of John of Gaunt, and the *Royal Cloister* with its beautiful Manueline tracery. Now it is only a few km to Portugal's other famous abbey at

ALCOBAÇA (372 km); the great church (1152) contains the lovely Gothic *tombs* of King Pedro I and Ines de Castro. The *sacristy* and the *chapel* opposite have an exceptional pair of Manueline doorways. From here you can make a detour (12 km) to the picturesque fishing village of *Nazare.*

Soon after *Alcobaça* is the *Pousada* (🏨) at *Alfeizerão.* We leave N1 at *Caldas da Rainha* for the little medieval walled city of *Obidos;* its *Pousada* (🏨), dating from 1375, is within the highest part of the old walls, originally built by the Moors. We continue by N8 through *Torres Vedras,* of Wellington fame, and over the last few hilly miles to

LISBON (489 km; pop. 784,000), the capital of Portugal, situated at the mouth of the R. *Tagus* on many steep hills overlooking one of the most beautiful harbours in the world. Much of the old city was destroyed by the great earthquake of 1755, but the medieval *St George's Castle* (fine view) and the Romanesque *cathedral* still stand. Other sights: (1) the lovely 18th-c. waterside *'Black Horse Square';* (2) the *Avenida de Liberdad,* the main street; (3) the *Janelas Verdes,* containing Lisbon's Art Gallery; (4) the churches of *São Vicente de Fora, Madre de Deus* (Manueline, tiled nave), *Estrêla* with its two domed towers, and *São Roque* (18th c., richly decorated).

Just outside the town at *Belem* is the *Convent of the Jerominos,* with its perfect Manueline *cloisters.* Nearby is the fairy-tale *Belem Tower* jutting out into the river, and the *Riding School* containing the famous collection of 'golden' coaches.

The Tower of Belem at Lisbon

Excursions: (1) the 'international' seaside resort of *Estoril* (18 km); (2) the lovely Rococo country palace of *Queluz* (1758–94) with its beautiful formal gardens; (3) *Sintra* (26 km), with its interesting old Palace (14th–17th c.; magnificent views).

🚇 (1) Coimbra–Oporto. (2) Castelo Branco–Guarda. (3) Merida–Madrid.

🏨 Avenida Palace, Rue 1º de Dezembro 123. 🏨 Europa, Praca de Louis de Camoes 6. 🏛 Francfort, Praca de D. Pedro IV 113.

Now we cross the *Tagus* by ferry, and the character of the country immediately changes. We pass *Azeitão* and the 15th-c. *Quinta de Bacalhoa,* and soon reach

SETUBAL (533 km), where the fortress was built by Philip II and the *Church of Jesus* (1491) has twisted Manueline pillars. Shortly after, the main road to *Madrid* turns left and you can follow it and N14 for a long detour to the ancient city of

EVORA (2nd-c. Roman *temple,* 12th-c. *cathedral, museum,* Roman *aqueduct, old walls,* and many interesting *churches*), rejoining the main road to Seville at

BEJA (671 km). Founded by Julius Caesar, it has a Roman *gate,* a Visigothic *church,* and a 14th-c. *castle.* From here a long drive, crossing the R. *Guadiana,* the frontier, and the *Sierra Morena,* brings us to

SEVILLE (898 km; see tour 7).